F

HAPPY 10th MONTH

LLUS

THE BEATLES
ON RECORD

MARK WALLGREN

A FIRESIDE BOOK
PUBLISHED BY SIMON AND SCHUSTER
NEW YORK

A Fireside Book
Published by Simon & Schuster, Inc.
Simon & Schuster Building
Rockefeller Center
1230 Avenue of the Americas
New York, New York 10020
FIRESIDE and colophon are registered trademarks of Simon & Schuster, Inc.
Designed by Jennie Nichols/Levavi & Levavi
Manufactured in the United States of America
10   9   8   7   6   5   4   3   2
Library of Congress Cataloging in Publication Data
Wallgren, Mark.
    The Beatles on record.

    "A Fireside book."
    Includes index.
    1. Beatles—Discography.   I. Title.
ML156.7.B4W3 1982   016.7899'12454'00922 82-10305
ISBN 0-671-45682-2

FOREWORD

Welcome to *THE BEATLES ON RECORD*. In this book you will find each and every single, EP, and album by the Beatles as a group and on their own as individual artists, as released commercially in the United States between 1962 and 1982. Every record has its own separate entry, which includes a full illustration of the record, a full review of the record, all historical technical data for the record (title, artist, label, catalog number, release date)—all of which is topped off by the official peak chart position as surveyed by all three major American record charts: *Billboard, Cash Box,* and *Record World*.

The book is divided into separate sections covering, in chronological order of release, the singles and the albums. In addition, special appendices have been included that cover non-charting reissues, records of special interest, and albums that include one or more Beatles tracks but are otherwise not considered actual Beatles albums, and worldwide chart totals. Also included are final appendices that serve as quick-reference chart supplements and grand total sections for the United States, as well as sections covering worldwide chart supplements.

THE CHARTS

The Beatles' dominance of the American record charts during their entire career, especially as a group in the sixties, but also on their own in the seventies, has now been fully documented and offered for your inspection and evaluation. The charts make for interesting reading and study, as many people are already aware. For those unaware, this book will open to you this unique and important aspect of the Beatles' impact for the past two decades on the American music scene.

In the United States, we have three major record industry trade publications that provide official weekly record charts: *Billboard, Cash Box,* and *Record World*. It is their job to reflect and report accurately on the popularity of the sounds that shape our lives. Each publication has its own methods for gathering and computing the exact figures and totals and resultant positions awarded to each record surveyed. With the thousands of new releases each year, this is clearly no small or easy task.

Roughly speaking, a record's ranking is based on a complex combination of its sales and airplay. The three charts differ slightly in the importance placed on each of these areas in determining a record's weekly chart placement.

Sometimes all three charts are in exact agreement. At other times, they may differ ever so slightly—or perhaps by a substantial margin. This is part of what makes following the charts so intriguing. Which one is right? Which one is off? How could one be off so much more than the other two? How could all three be so far apart in their tallies? That's all part of the fun.

Billboard, Cash Box, and *Record World** are very special and important publications.

---

*Unfortunately, *Record World* ceased publication following its issue dated April 10, 1982.

5

Although each is listed as a newspaper, the actual format tends to resemble that of a large magazine. In any case, they are the life and breath of the record industry, providing the music business with the same make-'em-or-break-'em weekly information that the various television ratings provide to the television industry. Thus, the charts have helped to make many stars—as well as break many stars.

A-SIDES/B-SIDES

Normally, a single (45 rpm) record is referred to as having an A-side, the hit, and a B-side, usually just a song whose only purpose is to fill the space on the other side of the hit. Due to the superb quality of the Beatles' material in general, quite often the B-sides of their singles were also played a great deal along with the hit A-sides, and were actually charted as well.

In the past, the B-side was charted separately from the A-side. Thus, it was possible for the same record to occupy the No. 3 and No. 86 positions simultaneously. This practice of splitting up the sides as separate chart entries lasted until 1969, when following the release of the Beatles' "Something"/"Come Together" single, all three charts adopted the practice of listing both sides as one combined entry if both sides were considered hits. This created, in effect, double A-sided singles. With few exceptions, all three charts have continued this procedure to date.

For the period when B-sides were charted separately (for the Beatles, this covers 1962–1969), the highest position reached for each B-side has been noted in the review section of the release. The position listed at the bottom of the page is for the A-side, and considered to be representative of the combined achievement for that disc.

TECHNICAL DATA

Underneath the illustration of each record is listed the title, artist, record label, catalog number, and original release date. The date of release noted is generally the official release date as given by the record company. However, on occasion the actual date a record is available on the market differs from the date targeted by the record company. In these instances, both dates have been given. The first date shown is the *actual* date of release to the public (when the record was first available in the stores for purchase), and the date shown in parentheses is the originally *scheduled* release date.

Differences in dates occur for a variety of reasons: various delays at the pressing plant or warehouse; changes needed so as to coincide with scheduled advertising in the trade publications; withholding of shipments to the stores for the purpose of allowing additional radio exposure in order to create increased buyer anticipation and demand; unexpected early completion of the discs, labels, or sleeves prior to the date originally scheduled.

To best determine the accuracy of the release-date information given, several sources have been checked and cross-referenced. The final dates listed are intended to provide the reader with the most reliable dates available.

THE REVIEWS

Each review attempts to point out facts of interest; accounts of the critics' and the public's response; radio airplay exposure at the time of release; and occasional interesting additional chart information.

As for comments regarding chart positions, it is important to point out that the Beatles, as you will see, are in a very special class. With the hundreds of new records released each week, it is certainly considered an honor in its own right even to chart among the Top 200 albums or Top 100 singles. However, as with anything concerning the Beatles, the stakes as well as the expectations have always been higher. From time to time in some of the reviews, a record has been referred to as having "failed" on the charts. This is largely based on the particular degree of expectation for each release. Thus, a single immediately picked to be a shoo-in for Top Five status that eventually stalls out at No. 18 might be referred to as a "failure." But keep in mind that this is only in terms of the *higher-than-normal standards applied to the Beatles' product,* both as a group and on their own. For other artists, a Top Twenty hit is by all means a success. It's just that the Beatles for so long seemed to hit Number One with nearly everything they did that people naturally expect more of the same from them, even as individual performers.

When you examine the Beatles' remarkable chart record you will see that their achievements and success as a group and as solo performers are wholly unparalleled in the history of the music business—and you will also see that not only have they no peers, but the likes of the Beatles will probably never be seen again.

TABLE OF CONTENTS

THE
BEATLES
ON RECORD

THE SINGLES

1962-1982

MY BONNIE/
  The Saints
Tony Sheridan and the Beat Brothers (THE BEATLES)

Decca 31382
April 23, 1962

This was the very first Beatles record to be released in America, in this case with them performing as the back-up band for singer Tony Sheridan, and credited as the Beat Brothers. This was of course Sheridan's single, and is noted here mainly because two years later, in 1964, it would resurface and be pushed as a Beatles disc. As for this go-round in 1962, it didn't do anything in the way of radio airplay or chart interest.

(It should be pointed out that this was the only time that the Beatles were credited under the name the Beat Brothers. All subsequent reissues of the material recorded with Sheridan in Hamburg, 1961, would be credited as "The Beatles featuring Tony Sheridan." Additional material released in following years and credited as "Tony Sheridan and the Beat Brothers" did *not* feature the Beatles, but, rather, other musicians under the guise of the Beat Brothers.)

Billboard

CASH BOX

Record World

PLEASE PLEASE ME/
Ask Me Why
THE BEATLES

Vee Jay 498
February 25, 1963

When the Beatles signed with the EMI recording organization in 1962, the agreement called for their records to be distributed in England on EMI's Parlophone label. It also gave EMI the rights to offer the Beatles material around the world, which it usually offered first to its many own labels located in nearly every free country on the planet.

Therefore, EMI's American arm, Capitol Records, was given the initial option of issuing the group's work in the United States. Capitol chose to pass on the quartet, as did several other record companies before Vee Jay Records finally agreed to release the Beatles' American debut product.

In spite of the fact that in England this disc was topping the charts, "Please Please Me" failed to please please anyone on this side of the Atlantic, generating no real radio interest, very little in terms of sales, and absolutely no chart action.

Billboard	CASH BOX	Record World

FROM ME TO YOU/
Thank You Girl
THE BEATLES

Vee Jay 522
May 27, 1963

If at first you don't succeed . . . Vee Jay tried once more to interest the American public in the newest British phenomenon by releasing the group's latest single, which of course was already sitting atop the English charts.

The response was just barely better this time around, with limited airplay in a few markets, and enough minor sales eventually to allow the record to creep onto *Billboard*'s chart and bubble under the Top 100 for a brief few weeks.

Billboard

CASH BOX

Record World

SHE LOVES YOU/
  I'll Get You
THE BEATLES

Swan 4152
September 16, 1963

Having gone nowhere with the Beatles' first two singles in America, Vee Jay passed on their next offering, and it eventually wound its way onto the Swan label.

Though it took nearly four months to catch on, this single became one of the group's all-time biggest hits in the United States, gaining enormous saturation-level airplay by early 1964, and rising to the top of the charts. There is probably not a more famous chorus in the history of popular music than this disc's "Yeah Yeah Yeah."

Billboard

CASH BOX

1

Record World

1

ROLL OVER BEETHOVEN/
Please Mr. Postman
THE BEATLES

Capitol of Canada 72133
December 9, 1963

Upon the initial wave of Beatlemania in early 1964, thirst for "new" Beatles material was so fierce in the United States that Beatles product from Canada was imported to help meet the overwhelming demand. This was one of two singles on Capitol's Canadian label to be imported and sold in huge enough quantities actually to place on the American charts.

During the first few months of 1964, one couldn't turn on the radio without hearing the lads from Liverpool on every station singing all their tunes. Undoubtedly, this is one which was heard among the rest.

68

CASH BOX

30

Record World

35

I WANT TO HOLD YOUR HAND/
I Saw Her Standing There
THE BEATLES

Capitol 5112
December 26, 1963 (January 13, 1964)

EMI decided it was time for the Beatles to capture the giant U.S. marketplace, so in an all-out effort to ensure total success for the group that had turned Great Britain upside down during all of 1963, EMI authorized its American firm, Capitol Records, to launch the largest promotional campaign in music business history.

The campaign was a whopping success, and from the moment it was released this record shot to the top of the charts and onto every radio wavelength in the nation. It would go on to become the biggest record of the year, and hold up as one of the Beatles' all-time biggest sellers.

While the A-side topped all three charts, only *Billboard* charted the B-side, raising it as high as No. 14 on its own.

Billboard

CASH BOX
(1)

Record World
[1]

MY BONNIE/
  The Saints
THE BEATLES featuring Tony Sheridan

MGM K13213
January 27, 1964

MGM, which had acquired four of the eight tunes from the Beatles' back-up sessions for singer Tony Sheridan in Hamburg, 1961, decided to make them pay off. This was done by rereleasing Polydor's 1962 Tony Sheridan single and capitalizing on the fact that the Beatles perform as the back-up group. Whereas the Polydor single had correctly identified the single as being by "Tony Sheridan and the Beat Brothers," MGM recredited it as "The Beatles Featuring Tony Sheridan." The record was rushed out in a picture sleeve prominently displaying the Beatles' name in an effort to pass this off as a real Beatles release, making for a sure-fire quick-seller before most people would stop and realize that the voice on both sides of this disc actually belongs to Sheridan.

The trick worked just long enough for the single to rise to the Top Thirty—before buyers caught on and then passed up this curious but meaningless-to-the-ears record.

26

CASH BOX

Record World

31

PLEASE PLEASE ME/
   From Me to You
THE BEATLES

Vee Jay 581
January 30, 1964

As the initial surge of Beatlemania began to increase, Vee Jay jumped back into the singles' race by coupling the two A-sides from their 1963 efforts and issuing them together on one disc.

"Please Please Me," which had been totally ignored almost a full year earlier, now became a top hit smash seller that immediately secured twenty-four-hour airplay and rose almost to the very top of the charts, being kept away only by other Beatles records already occupying the Number One position.

Cash Box again chose not to chart separately the B-side, this time "From Me To You," but the other two charts did, with *Billboard* peaking it at No. 41, and *Record World* getting it to No. 46.

CASH BOX

3

ALL MY LOVING/
   This Boy
THE BEATLES

Capitol of Canada 72144
February 17, 1964

Another of the imported Capitol of Canada singles to flood the U.S. market in early 1964, this record sold enough copies to make its way onto the American charts, doing slightly better overall than the "Roll Over Beethoven" Canadian single also on the charts during the same period.

CASH BOX

(31)

Record World

32

TWIST AND SHOUT/
There's a Place
THE BEATLES

Tollie 9001
March 2, 1964

Prompted by the overwhelming success of their last single (the rereleased "Please Please Me"), Vee Jay soon rushed out yet another pair of tunes from their INTRODUCING THE BEATLES album. "Twist and Shout" was a raw and powerful cover version of the Isley Brothers' hit, with John Lennon delivering a truly savage lead vocal, one which he later said had permanently strained his vocal cords.

Vee Jay released the single on their Tollie label, and the record soon skyrocketed to the top of the charts, hitting Number One on *Record World* and *Cash Box*, while stopping at No. 2 on *Billboard*, all the while sandwiched between four other Beatles singles—the whole of the nation's Top Five. Again, only *Billboard* bothered charting the B-side, slipping it in as high as No. 74.

CASH BOX

Record World

1

CAN'T BUY ME LOVE/
  You Can't Do That
THE BEATLES

Capitol 5150
March 16, 1964 (March 30, 1964)

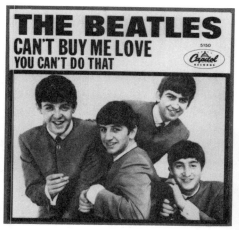

This was actually the next "official" Beatles single, and the second from Capitol. However, by the time this record was issued, almost a half-dozen singles on almost as many different labels had flooded the voracious Beatles market. Nonetheless, that did not keep this disc from setting the record for the most advance sales of a single in U.S. music industry history.

In addition to taking over the airwaves, this single also replaced other Beatles singles occupying the top position on all three of the charts. Once more, only *Billboard* continued the practice of separately charting the B-side, and placed "You Can't Do That" as high as No. 48.

1

CASH BOX

1

Record World

1

THE BEATLES (EP)
  Misery/A Taste of Honey//
  Ask Me Why/Anna
THE BEATLES

Vee Jay VJEP 1-903
March 23, 1964

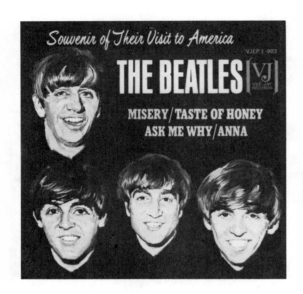

Vee Jay looked across the Atlantic to Great Britain and saw the huge success of the Beatles' EP's on the UK charts, and figured to duplicate that success Stateside. So, they took four songs from the INTRODUCING THE BEATLES album and issued them in the EP format, with a special cardboard picture cover.

Despite the claim that this EP sold more copies than either of the Capitol EP's that followed later (a claim that would appear to be backed up by the fact that of the three EP's this is by far and away the most easily found by record collectors, thus suggesting that more were sold), it failed to make any of the American record charts.

Part of the reason might have been in the marketing of the EP, which made it hard for the charts to report accurately. For a time, Vee Jay even sold this EP through the mail in conjunction with a potato chip company (buy the chips, send in the wrapper, get the record).

Billboard   CASH BOX   *Record World*

DO YOU WANT TO KNOW A SECRET/
Thank You Girl
THE BEATLES

Vee Jay 587
March 23, 1964

Released the same day as Vee Jay's EP of Beatles tunes, this single paired another selection from INTRODUCING THE BEATLES with the original B-side of the second Vee Jay Beatles single released in 1963.

In case no one had noticed, with the release of this new single and EP, Vee Jay had managed to reissue nearly all of the songs from their INTRODUCING THE BEATLES album in the 45 rpm format.

This record also gave George Harrison his very first A-side lead vocal, and it proved to be grandly successful, almost topping the charts. *Billboard* charted the B-side as high as No. 35, while *Record World* placed it at No. 39. *Cash Box* passed on it.

Billboard	CASH BOX	Record World
2	3	3

WHY/
  Cry for a Shadow
THE BEATLES featuring Tony Sheridan

MGM K13227
March 27, 1964

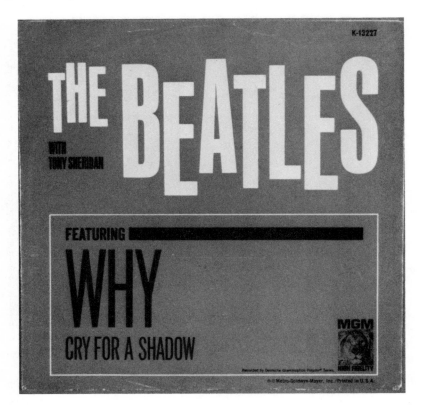

MGM took the two remaining Beatles/Sheridan tracks they owned (all four of which had by now been issued on their album THE BEATLES WITH TONY SHERIDAN AND THEIR GUESTS) and issued a second single, once again in a special picture sleeve (featuring identical artwork to their first, although this time in red, not green) that made certain to cash in on the Beatles' name.

By now, almost everyone had caught on to this farce, though it did place on *Billboard* briefly.

CASH BOX

Record World

LOVE ME DO/
P.S. I Love You
THE BEATLES

Tollie 9008
April 27, 1964

A year and a half after its original British debut and mild chart success, the Beatles' first full-fledged single was finally released in America. It quickly took off on a fast trip up the charts that didn't stop until "Love Me Do" had given the Beatles yet another Number One hit in the States.

With continued legal flak from Capitol, Vee Jay opted once more to place this "new" Beatles single on their Tollie label. Radio airplay was as universally heavy for this single as with any of their other Number One hits at the time. The B-side received a great deal of airplay as well, and this time all three charts rated it separately. "P.S. I Love You" rose to No. 10 on both *Cash Box* and *Billboard,* and to No. 13 on *Record World.*

Billboard

☆ 1

CASH BOX

① 1

Record World

1

FOUR BY THE BEATLES (EP)
    Roll Over Beethoven/All My Loving//
    This Boy/Please Mr. Postman
THE BEATLES

Capitol EAP-2121
May 11, 1964

Despite the recent chart failure and uncertain sales performance of the Vee Jay EP, Capitol decided to test American record buyers with the EP format by combining the two most successful Canadian import singles and issuing them together on this one disc.

Whether Americans just weren't interested in the EP format, or whether those that were already owned both of the Canadian import singles, the end result was a record that came and went with little success. It would not be until 1965 before Capitol would again try the EP format with Beatles fans.

Billboard

92

CASH BOX

86

Record World

—

SIE LIEBT DICH/
I'll Get You
THE BEATLES

Swan 4182
May 21, 1964

The Beatles had recently recorded "I Want to Hold Your Hand" and "She Loves You" in German, for release in Germany. Since Swan had owned only two Beatles songs, and one of them was, in fact, "She Loves You," they apparently had the rights to issue the German-sung version, which they gladly did. (Capitol got "Komm Gib Mir Diene Hand" and placed it on their SOMETHING NEW album.)

Predictably, the novelty didn't work, with very little airplay and even less in the way of sales, as evidenced by the minor chart action.

Billboard

97

CASH BOX

—

Record World

—

SWEET GEORGIA BROWN/
Take Out Some Insurance on Me Baby
THE BEATLES featuring Tony Sheridan

ATCO 6302
June 1, 1964

Like MGM, ATCO owned the rights to four of the 1961 Hamburg recordings with Tony Sheridan, thus allowing them to pull the same set of tricks that MGM had already pulled on the Beatles' record-buying public. However, the four tunes owned by ATCO were not the same four owned by MGM (there were eight in all).

Apparently, ATCO decided to test the waters, so to speak, by releasing this pair of Tony Sheridan-sung numbers as their initial Beatles product. As with the MGM singles, the label stated that the record was by "The Beatles featuring Tony Sheridan." Radio programmers were not fooled, and neither was the public, and this disc deservedly dropped out of sight upon release.

32

AIN'T SHE SWEET/
Nobody's Child
THE BEATLES
(B-side: THE BEATLES featuring Tony Sheridan)

ATCO 6308
July 6, 1964

On their second try, ATCO didn't take any chances. This time out, they issued their single in a picture sleeve displaying not only the Beatles' name, but also a drawing of four mop-top heads, obviously in an attempt to boost sales. It worked, but mainly because this single featured the only song from the 1961 Hamburg sessions actually to be sung by the Beatles—in this case, a young and raw John Lennon carrying the lead vocal on "Ain't She Sweet."

Why ATCO had not issued this as their initial single is not clear, though perhaps they were a bit wary of the legal action and lawsuits from Capitol Records in the air at the time.

In any case, though sounding a bit primitive compared with their new releases at the time, it worked well enough on the radio and at the sales counter to give ATCO and the Beatles a Top Twenty hit.

Billboard

19

CASH BOX

14

Record World

13

A HARD DAY'S NIGHT/
I Should Have Known Better
THE BEATLES

Capitol 5222
July 13, 1964

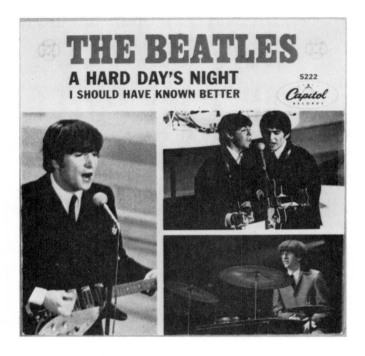

Two weeks after United Artists had already released the soundtrack album, Capitol issued this title-track single. Needless to say, coinciding with the release of the group's first major motion picture, this record swiftly climbed the charts, and didn't put on the brakes until it had given Capitol its third straight Number One Beatles single.

It seemed as though the passing of every couple of months meant that there would be a brand new Beatles single that would dominate the radio programming of all pop stations across America. Beatlemania continued in full bloom, and at this point, midway through 1964, it seemed that it would never let up.

Only *Billboard* separately charted the B-side, which it raised as high as No. 53.

 CASH BOX

1   1   1

I'LL CRY INSTEAD/
I'm Happy Just to Dance with You
THE BEATLES

Capitol 5234
July 20, 1964

One week after the release of the "A Hard Day's Night" single, Capitol attempted to cash in further on the motion picture by simultaneously issuing two additional singles comprised of other songs featured in the movie's soundtrack.

Despite the fact that "I'll Cry Instead" received saturation-level airplay on the radio, this single failed to do as well as expected. Perhaps the biggest strike against it was the fact that the song was cut from the film, and suffered from lack of theater exposure. In truth, though, probably Capitol had simply dumped *too much* product on the market all at once (three singles plus an album with songs from the movie, all *after* most fans had already purchased the soundtrack album on United Artists). Whatever the reasons, this record failed to make the Top Twenty, giving Capitol its first Beatles single not to hit Number One.

Billboard slipped the B-side onto the charts just long enough to let it barely climb into the Top 100, getting as high as No. 95, while *Record World* and *Cash Box* passed on it.

Billboard

25

CASH BOX

22

Record World

28

AND I LOVE HER/IF I FELL
THE BEATLES

Capitol 5235
July 20, 1964

This was the second of two new Capitol Beatles singles released on the same day. Both sides were quickly added to the radio station playlists all across America and were heard around the clock. Nonetheless, this record also failed for Capitol, falling short of the Top Ten on all three charts. Reasons for this are basically the same as those for the "I'll Cry Instead" single, though Capitol surely would have expected a single featuring a pair of love ballads, one sung by John and one by Paul, to seduce many more sales.

Interesting to note here is that *Billboard* and *Record World* charted both sides, giving "And I Love Her" as the A-side. "If I Fell" was delegated the B-side and rose to No. 53 on *Billboard,* and No. 59 on *Record World.* Meanwhile, *Cash Box* considered "If I Fell" to be the A-side, and did not list "And I Love Her" at all.

Billboard

12

CASH BOX

14

Record World

16

MATCHBOX/SLOW DOWN
THE BEATLES

Capitol 5255
August 24, 1964

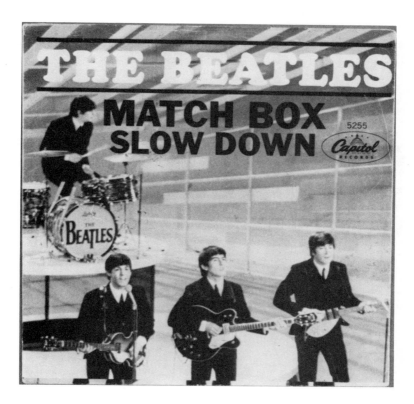

For their next single, Capitol pulled this pair of cover versions off the SOMETHING NEW album and released them as a double A-side offering.

Both sides performed fairly well, though it was obvious that this material did not quite live up to the quality of songs that the Beatles had been writing for themselves by this point in 1964, and the single stalled out before getting close to the Top Ten.

All three charts wound up with "Matchbox" on top, while the flip side, "Slow Down," rose to No. 23 on *Record World,* No. 25 on *Billboard,* and No. 34 on *Cash Box.*

Billboard

⭐ **17**

CASH BOX

(**17**)

Record World

| **22** |

I FEEL FINE/
She's a Woman
THE BEATLES

Capitol 5327
November 23, 1964

The Beatles' Christmas-season single for 1964 was yet another step forward in the progress of their music. "I Feel Fine" once again offered a brand new sound from the Fab Four, who even went so far as to start the record off with feedback—another rock 'n' roll first!

This disc allowed the Beatles to end the year in the same fashion they had begun it, with a Number One single, which in this case was helped along on its trek up the charts by a very strong B-side, which was charted on its own as high as No. 4 on *Billboard*, and as high as No. 8 on both *Cash Box* and *Record World*.

Billboard   CASH BOX   *Record World*

☆ 1   ① 1 | 1 |

4 BY THE BEATLES (EP)
Honey Don't/I'm a Loser//
Everybody's Trying to Be My Baby/Mr. Moonlight
THE BEATLES

Capitol R-5365
February 1, 1965

For their first Beatles release of 1965, Capitol once again tried the EP format out on American Beatles fans, and once again, the public failed to go for the idea, although this disc did somewhat better than the Beatles' previous EP nine months earlier. Nonetheless, Capitol abandoned the EP format for the Beatles thereafter.

On the charts, *Cash Box* and *Billboard* agreed on its mild success, while *Record World* thought otherwise.

68

CASH BOX

68

—

EIGHT DAYS A WEEK/
   I Don't Want to Spoil the Party
THE BEATLES

Capitol 5371
February 15, 1965

The Beatles' first single of 1965 provided them with yet another Number One hit. "Eight Days a Week" also continued the musical innovation and growth of the group, evidenced by the fact that this record began with a fade-in. The Beatles explained that since most records normally fade out at the end, they felt it might be interesting to fade in at the start!

Apparently the public agreed, as this record sped right to the top of all three charts, and received saturation-level airplay on the radio. Only *Billboard* charted the B-side, raising it to No. 39.

Billboard

CASH BOX

(1)

Record World

1

TICKET TO RIDE/
Yes It Is
THE BEATLES

Capitol 5407
April 19, 1965

Although things were not as hectic and confusing as they were in the first half of 1964, mainly because the Beatles were now appearing on only one label (Capitol), the demand for new records from the group continued strong into 1965.

This single was issued as a preview to the upcoming HELP album and motion picture, though at the time of its release the film's original working title, *Eight Arms to Hold You,* was placed on the record's label (and remained there—through four additional label variations—before finally being removed in 1981.)

Universal saturation on the radio for this one, and the Beatles had their third straight Number One single. *Billboard* charted the B-side, "Yes It Is," and saw that it got to No. 46.

CASH BOX

Record World

1

1

1

HELP!/
I'm Down
THE BEATLES

Capitol 5476
July 19, 1965

"Help!" became the cry of the summer of 1965, as the Beatles released their newest single, followed soon by the album and motion picture of the same title (having all been changed from *Eight Arms to Hold You*—thank goodness!).

"Help!" performed in true Beatles fashion, quickly rising to the top of the charts. Again, radio response was immediate and overwhelming, and this John Lennon lead-sung rocker was so well crafted musically and commercially that it would not be until much later that the important lyrics of the song became recognized and understood.

At the time, *Billboard* bubbled the B-side, "I'm Down," only as high as No. 101, while one hundred positions away the A-side held down the top position on all three charts. Incidentally, "I'm Down" would somehow manage to elude inclusion on any Beatles album until the 1976 ROCK 'N' ROLL MUSIC repackage.

Billboard
☆ 1

CASH BOX
① 1

Record World
1

YESTERDAY/
  Act Naturally
THE BEATLES

Capitol 5498
September 13, 1965

For the Beatles' next single, Capitol pulled from the British HELP album two tracks that had been omitted from the U.S. soundtrack compilation. The selection was definitely a wise one, as this solo McCartney ballad soon became one of the group's all-time biggest hits, and the composition itself became the most rerecorded of any Beatles tune ever.

Interesting sidenote is that Parlophone in England thought it was just another album track, so there was no UK single released at the time. Eleven years later, in 1976, it would finally emerge in Britain as a single and go on to make the Top Ten.

In the fall of 1965, "Yesterday" mastered the airwaves of America's radio stations and easily topped the charts. *Cash Box* joined *Billboard* in charting the B-side, going so far as to put Ringo's "Act Naturally" as high as No. 28, while *Billboard* placed it as high as No. 47.

Billboard

☆ 1

CASH BOX

① 1

Record World

1

BOYS/KANSAS CITY
THE BEATLES

Capitol Starline 6066
October 11, 1965

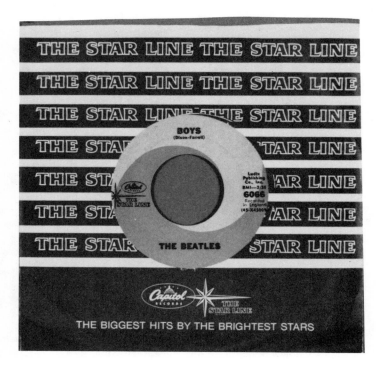

In the fall of 1965, Capitol reissued the four Vee Jay singles from 1964, along with two new couplings, via their Starline "oldies" label. Besides this disc, the other "new" single was "Misery"/"Roll Over Beethoven" (see Appendix). Actually, Capitol had hoped to make "Boys"/"Kansas City" a full-fledged Beatles release, but Brian Epstein and the Beatles objected, no longer wishing to issue "old" material as "new" singles product.

Of the six Starline singles, this was the only one that managed to catch on for a few weeks, being played in various radio markets around the States as the "new" Beatles single, which allowed it to slip onto the charts. Only *Cash Box* charted the B-side, "Kansas City," ranking it just behind the A-side on their chart at No. 75.

Billboard

102

CASH BOX

73

Record World

—

WE CAN WORK IT OUT/DAY TRIPPER
THE BEATLES

Capitol 5555
December 6, 1965

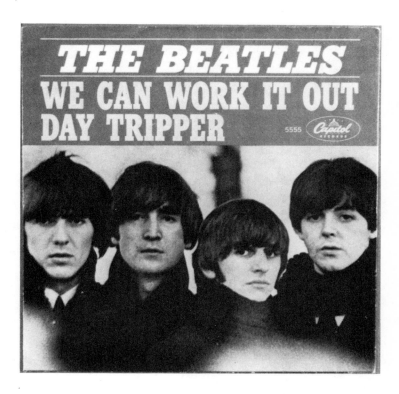

Perhaps one of the strongest double A-side couplings in the history of the record industry, this disc soon followed the typical Beatles pattern of shooting right to the top of the charts.

Strategically issued just in time for the Christmas season, this single quickly received saturation-level airplay for both sides, though the record charts eventually split them up and gave "We Can Work It Out" top honors. The equally impressive "Day Tripper" was ranked as high as No. 5 by *Billboard,* No. 10 by *Cash Box,* and No. 15 by *Record World.* The charts agreed on "We Can Work It Out"—and gave the Beatles their sixth consecutive Number One single (not counting the Capitol EP or Starline singles).

Billboard

☆ 1

CASH BOX

① 1

Record World

1

NOWHERE MAN/
What Goes On
THE BEATLES

Capitol 5587
February 21, 1966 (February 7, 1966)

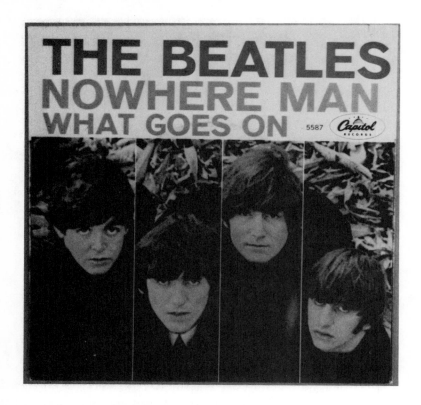

For the Beatles' first U.S. single of 1966, Capitol selected from the UK RUBBER SOUL album a pair of tunes that had been left off the American release.

"Nowhere Man" quickly performed in standard Beatles manner as it immediately soaked the airwaves and headed right up the charts. However, only *Record World* proclaimed this disc as receiving its deservedly Number One status. *Cash Box* and *Billboard* seemed just a pinch unsure and stalled the record just short of the top spot on each. *Billboard* also charted the B-side, "What Goes On," as high as No. 81.

Billboard	CASH BOX	Record World
☆ 3	②	1

PAPERBACK WRITER/
Rain
THE BEATLES

Capitol 5651
May 23, 1966

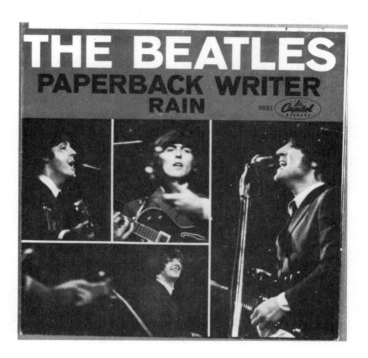

The Beatles' second single for 1966 rewarded them with yet another Number One placing, and deservedly so. "Paperback Writer" was a very fast-paced rocker with catchy lead guitar licks and ultra-heavy bass notes. Even the B-side, "Rain," was drenched with McCartney's bass guitar in a way no other Beatles recording had been to date, helping to create still another single which showcased another new sound for the group.

Radio airplay was very heavy for this single, and up to normal saturation level in most markets. In addition, *Billboard* saw "Rain" get as high as No. 23, while *Cash Box* placed it as high as No. 31. Unanimous agreement this time over the Number One status of the A-side.

Billboard

☆ 1

CASH BOX

① 1

Record World

1

YELLOW SUBMARINE/ELEANOR RIGBY
THE BEATLES

Capitol 5715
August 5, 1966

This single was pulled from the group's new album, REVOLVER, and, like the album, this single was a marked departure in musical style for the Beatles—a departure that served to fuel claims of the group's genius and inventiveness.

For all intents and purposes, this was a double A-sided hit, though the charts made certain that "Eleanor Rigby" performed on its own as the B-side. *Billboard* had it just miss the Top Ten, coming in at No. 11, while *Cash Box* placed it as high as No. 12 and *Record World* at No. 16. As for the A-side, *Record World* and *Cash Box* awarded the Beatles yet another Number One single, while *Billboard* found the Beatles failing to hit the top of their chart for the second time in 1966.

Billboard

☆ 2

CASH BOX

(1)

Record World

[1]

PENNY LANE/STRAWBERRY FIELDS FOREVER
THE BEATLES

Capitol 5810
February 13, 1967

The Beatles

The Beatles opened 1967 with their most unique sounding single so far. In addition to their new musical sound, they also had a new appearance, as evidenced by the photo on the record's picture sleeve.

Even so, while the Fab Four was obviously growing up, so was their audience, and this single was another unqualified double A-sided hit, though under the old system of listing each track separately, the equally good, if not better, "Strawberry Fields Forever" was made to perform as the B-side, rising to No. 8 on *Billboard,* No. 9 on *Record World,* and just missing the Top Ten on *Cash Box* at No. 11. The more commercial-sounding pop hit, "Penny Lane," left no doubt on any chart, and radio airplay was again at saturation level.

Billboard

CASH BOX

Record World

1

ALL YOU NEED IS LOVE/
Baby You're a Rich Man
THE BEATLES

Capitol 5964
July 24, 1967

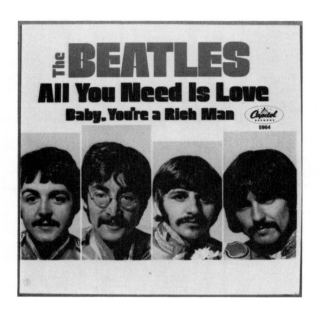

SGT. PEPPER had helped to launch the summer of love, and this new Beatles single was undoubtedly meant to serve as the national anthem for flower children everywhere. Stated so simply and beautifully, the record's message served only to cement further the Beatles' standing as the Number One spokesmen and representatives for their generation.

The song was written especially for the *Our World* television special broadcast live worldwide, which featured the Beatles recording the song in their London studios. The finished single was rushed out to the stores very soon thereafter.

Radio airplay was again at saturation level, and the only thing higher than this record on the charts at the time was many of the people listening to it. On its own, the B-side performed well enough to get to No. 34 on *Billboard,* No. 60 on *Record World,* and No. 65 on *Cash Box.*

Billboard	CASH BOX	Record World
		1

HELLO GOODBYE/
I Am the Walrus
THE BEATLES

Capitol 2056
November 27, 1967

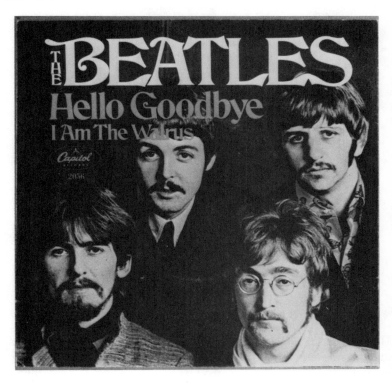

The Beatles closed out 1967 with their third Number One single of the year. The A-side was a nice pop rocker, "Hello Goodbye," while the B-side, "I Am the Walrus," was again considered by many as not only equal to the A-side, but perhaps superior as well. Nonetheless, the record performed in the same manner as the two previous singles of 1967 had, with this disc soon resting on top of the charts.

Airplay was extremely heavy, and to saturation level in most markets. *Cash Box* noted "I Am the Walrus" doing as well as No. 46 on its own, while *Billboard* placed it as high as No. 56. All three charts agreed on the A-side.

Billboard

☆ 1

CASH BOX

(1)

Record World

| 1 |

LADY MADONNA/
The Inner Light
THE BEATLES

Capitol 2138
March 18, 1968

The Beatles' first single of 1968 found the group returning to an almost fifties-flavored rock 'n' roll sound with this McCartney-sung Elvis impression driven by a pounding piano beat. Perhaps after all of the psychedelic sounds of 1967, the public found this offering a bit too simplistic. In retrospect, the group indeed might have had more success with the original version of John's "Across the Universe," which was recorded at the same time and was originally slated to be the A-side of this record, but was switched at the last minute and replaced with "Lady Madonna."

Nevertheless, "Lady Madonna" performed quite well, although radio airplay dipped slightly in some markets this time around. *Billboard* found the transcendental B-side, "The Inner Light," only enlightening enough to raise it as high as No. 96, while the other two charts passed on it. On the A-side, the Beatles' new release almost topped two of charts.

Billboard

CASH BOX

Record World | 2 |

HEY JUDE/
  Revolution
THE BEATLES

Apple 2276
August 26, 1968

Under their new contract with EMI, all Beatles records would henceforth be issued on their own Apple Records label. In America, Capitol would distribute Apple, thus retaining their most valuable clients.

For their initial Apple offering, the Beatles produced what would turn out to be their all-time biggest hit single. "Hey Jude" was a monster-sized success, from its unheard-of seven-minute-plus running time to its lengthy stay on top of the charts at Number One.

The B-side, "Revolution," was a giant of a hit in its own right, and undoubtedly was responsible for a good deal of the total record-setting number of copies sold of this disc. It was charted as high as No. 2 on its own by *Record World,* and No. 12 by *Billboard.*

Billboard   CASH BOX   *Record World*
1   1   1

GET BACK/
   Don't Let Me Down
THE BEATLES

Apple 2490
May 5, 1969

For their first new single of 1969, the Beatles chose the only song which was, self-admittedly, the only "finished" number to result from their January recording/film sessions. It was also to be the title track of the GET BACK album and television special reportedly due to follow soon.

Even though that would not be the final case, "Get Back" itself was a pounding McCartney rocker that further returned the Beatles to basic rock 'n' roll. It quickly soared to the top of all three U.S. charts, and achieved domination and saturation of America's transistor radios.

Only *Billboard* bothered to chart separately the B-side, raising Lennon's beautiful love song, "Don't Let Me Down," as high as No. 35.

CASH BOX

Record World

1

54

THE BALLAD OF JOHN AND YOKO/
Old Brown Shoe
THE BEATLES

Apple 2531
June 4, 1969 (June 16, 1969)

Just one month after the release of the new "Get Back" single, the Beatles rush released yet another new single, which entered the charts while "Get Back" was topping them.

"The Ballad of John and Yoko" told the story-in-song of John and Yoko's latest escapades, and moved along quite nicely in true pop rocker fashion, with Lennon describing it at the time as "Johnny B. Paperback Writer." However, the use of the line "Christ, you know it ain't easy" in the song's chorus was taken as offensive by many radio stations in America, and subsequently was banned on all but a handful of them, thus severely limiting the airplay of the disc. Since the U.S. charts are based on a combination of sales *and* radio airplay, this affected the single's performance and kept it in the lower half of the Top Ten on all three charts.

Billboard 8

CASH BOX 10

Record World 7

GIVE PEACE A CHANCE/
Remember Love
PLASTIC ONO BAND

Apple 1809
July 7, 1969 (July 28, 1969)

The first solo single from any of the Beatles was John's initial venture under the Plastic Ono Band name. Wanting to provide the peace movement with a national anthem of its own, this record was quickly written and recorded in John and Yoko's hotel room in Montreal during the Canadian leg of their famous "bed-in" events.

The record was soon released, and because of the obvious Lennon vocals headed up the charts. However, by design, it was more of a chant than a true song and eventually radio airplay slowed down as did the single just as it neared the Top Ten.

Billboard

14

CASH BOX

11

Record World

10

SOMETHING/COME TOGETHER
THE BEATLES

Apple 2654
October 6, 1969 (October 13, 1969)

The Beatles' next single was this pair of tunes taken from the ABBEY ROAD album. George's composition was the first time a song of his own writing had made the A-side of a Beatles single, though it was John's song that ultimately pulled the disc to the top of the charts and qualified this record as a true double A-sided hit.

Radio airplay was at saturation level for both sides of this record, which performed quite unusually on the charts. *Billboard* and *Cash Box* listed the single as separate sides. *Cash Box* had "Come Together" reach Number One, while "Something" followed at No. 2. *Billboard* raised "Come Together" to No. 2 and "Something" to No. 3, then combined the two sides, and henceforth went with the belief that a record should be charted as a sole entry, regardless of whether it is a lone or double A-sided hit. *Billboard* then joined *Record World* in awarding "Come Together"/"Something" the Number One position.

COLD TURKEY/
Don't Worry Kyoko
PLASTIC ONO BAND

Apple 1813
October 20, 1969 (November 10, 1969)

John's second solo single was originally meant to be the Beatles' next single, but the other three turned thumbs down on it, so it became the second Plastic Ono Band single.

John's ripping vocal scream about the pain of drug withdrawal, combined with some ear-piercing guitar work, came a bit too close to relating accurately the symptoms of that experience for most of the public and radio programmers to feel at ease with. Thus, the disc did not receive the kind of airplay expected at this point for any of the Beatles records, whether as a group or as solo artists. After all, Beatle John's single "Come Together" was rising to the top of the charts at the same time this record barely skipped in and out of the Top Thirty.

Billboard	CASH BOX	Record World
30	32	26

INSTANT KARMA/
   Who Has Seen the Wind
JOHN ONO LENNON
   (B-side: Yoko Ono Lennon/Plastic Ono Band)

Apple 1818
February 20, 1970 (March 2, 1970)

John decided not to take any chances with his third solo single. Now that the Beatles were finished, he made certain there would be no guessing about whose record this was—dropping the Plastic Ono Band name in favor of his own.

Perhaps one of Lennon's greatest hits, this record soon became enormously popular, both with the public and the radio stations, which gave it a great amount of airplay and exposure. The song really deserved Number One status, but at the last crucial moment it was overtaken on the charts by the Beatles' own single, "Let It Be." Although the Beatles had blocked out their own records from the top spot several times before, this must have come as a heavy blow to John, on the verge of his biggest solo success so far.

Billboard   **CASH BOX**   **Record World**

☆ 3   (3)   [3]

LET IT BE/
   You Know My Name (Look Up the Number)
THE BEATLES

Apple 2764
March 11, 1970 (March 16, 1970)

After several months of changes and delays, the collection of songs originally recorded and filmed in January 1969 were finally about to be released. GET BACK seemed a bit dated by now, so the title of the album and the movie was changed to LET IT BE, which happened to be the title of the song that critics, upon hearing several test pressings of the album during 1969, had been picking for quite some time as the most likely next single.

This McCartney-sung ballad tested well in true "Hey Jude" fashion, and immediately climbed to the top of the charts, being responsible in part for keeping Lennon's solo single, "Instant Karma," from hitting the top spot itself. "Let It Be" would sell well enough to go on and become one of the Beatles' all-time biggest hits.

Billboard
1

CASH BOX
1

Record World
1

THE LONG AND WINDING ROAD/FOR YOU BLUE
THE BEATLES

Apple 2832
May 11, 1970 (May 25, 1970)

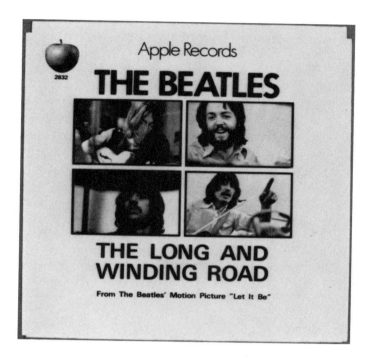

As the follow-up to "Let It Be," this pair of soundtrack tunes from the LET IT BE album were selected by Allen Klein as the next American Beatles single. It proved to be a smart choice, as this record instantly became a double A-sided smash hit, gaining a great deal of radio airplay for both McCartney's tender ballad and Harrison's skiffle-beat rocker.

Until reissued material would begin to be released in 1976, this would be the last Beatles single in the United States. It gave the Beatles their 23rd Number One single on *Record World,* their 22nd Number One single on *Cash Box,* and their 20th Number One single on *Billboard.* This amazing record was accomplished in a span of less than seven years.

Billboard

1

CASH BOX

1

Record World

1

BEAUCOUPS OF BLUES/
   Coochy-Coochy
RINGO STARR

Apple 2969/1826
October 5, 1970 (October 19, 1970)

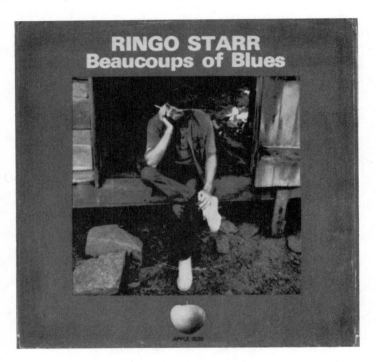

Ringo's first solo single was the title track from his country and western album, BEAU-COUPS OF BLUES. Because of his former-Beatle status, this strictly country and western number managed to cross over onto the pop charts, if only just barely.

There was virtually no airplay on the rock stations and little help from the country and western stations either, who didn't know what to do with a record by a former member of the world's most famous rock 'n' roll band.

Apple released the single with two different catalog numbers appearing both on labels and on the picture sleeve. (Apple later would go ahead and issue a Billy Preston single with the same 1826 number.)

Billboard

★ 87

CASH BOX

(69)

Record World

87

MY SWEET LORD/ISN'T IT A PITY
GEORGE HARRISON

Apple 2995
November 23, 1970

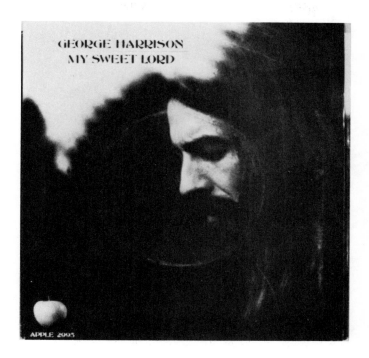

George's first solo single was this double A-sided hit consisting of religious celebration and achievement in "My Sweet Lord," and personal commentary and feelings about the breakup of the Beatles in "Isn't It a Pity."

This would prove to be the most successful solo single by any of the former Beatles during the seventies. This record shot up like lightning to the top of the charts (just in time for the Christmas holidays) and held on to the Number One spot well into the new year.

No doubt about it, Christmas 1970 belonged to former-Beatle George Harrison, and the radio airplay was at saturation level for both sides of this disc, while the charts were unanimous in their Number One ranking.

Billboard

☆ 1

CASH BOX

① 1

Record World

1

MOTHER/
Why
JOHN LENNON/PLASTIC ONO BAND
(B-side: Yoko Ono/Plastic Ono Band)

Apple 1827
December 28, 1970 (January 4, 1971)

John Lennon chose to release "Mother" as the single from his JOHN LENNON/PLAS-TIC ONO BAND album, even though he realized that the song "Love" would probably have made for a more commercially successful hit. Even so, he stuck with the highly personal and painful "Mother," trying to get a different and difficult message across to the public, most of whom he candidly admitted at the time would not care for or understand the song.

Reaction in the radio world of pop music was mixed, but it was clear that Lennon's observations had been correct. Airplay ranged from fair to poor, depending on the market, while the charts also seemed mixed in their accounts of the record's popularity, with *Record World* and *Cash Box* scoring the single as a Top Twenty hit, while *Billboard* had it fail to make the Top Forty.

Billboard

43

CASH BOX

19

Record World

16

WHAT IS LIFE/
Apple Scruffs
GEORGE HARRISON

Apple 1828
February 15, 1971 (February 8, 1971)

The second single pulled from the massive ALL THINGS MUST PASS album, "What Is Life," was a powerful and piercing rocker that featured some of George's hottest guitar licks on wax.

Reaction to the single was sudden and swift, and all in favor. There was heavy radio airplay for this one, though, perhaps because so many had already purchased the album, the sales lagged just enough to keep this from getting any closer to the top, and it had to settle for only Top Ten status.

Billboard

10

CASH BOX

7

Record World

10

ANOTHER DAY/OH WOMAN OH WHY
PAUL McCARTNEY

Apple 1829
February 22, 1971 (February 28, 1971)

Paul's first solo single came just less than a year after his debut solo album. This single was a double A-sided hit on all of the charts. "Another Day" was the sort of bubble-gum pop number for which Paul would continually receive the wrath of the critics and sometimes even of the public for many years to follow. While "Oh Woman Oh Why," on the other hand, featured Paul's ripping-vocal rocking side that so many wished he would display more often.

Actually, it was "Oh Woman Oh Why" that gained the most initial radio airplay, though as time went on "Another Day" usually was heard most often. Surprisingly, even with two sides going for him, Paul failed to hit the top spot on the charts, edged out by the likes of Three Dog Night's "Joy to the World" and similar fare.

Billboard	CASH BOX	Record World
5	6	5

POWER TO THE PEOPLE/
Touch Me
JOHN LENNON/PLASTIC ONO BAND
(B-side: Yoko Ono/Plastic Ono Band)

Apple 1830
March 22, 1971 (April 29, 1971)

With this record John tried to rebound from the slight drop in his solo singles career caused by the less than universal appeal of "Mother." He put another favorite protest slogan to music, hoping to create another new anthem for the young and restless generation.

This non-album single very strongly pushed the highly political phrase "Power to the People," but nevertheless gained a fairly large amount of radio airplay. It became quite popular, managing to return John to the Top Ten, more or less.

11

CASH BOX

10

Record World

8

IT DON'T COME EASY/
Early 1970
RINGO STARR

Apple 1831
April 16, 1971 (April 14, 1971)

Ringo's first rock 'n' roll single was a superb smash hit for the ex-Beatle not expected to accomplish anything worthwhile in music on his own. Featuring fellow ex-Beatle George Harrison as producer/guitarist, it almost could have been called "Ringo's Theme Part 2," as the lyrics rang quite autobiographical.

The record laid the foundation for Ringo's reign during the first half of the seventies as a solid hit singles artist. The charts were almost unanimous in their treatment of this justifiably Number One effort.

Billboard
☆ 4

CASH BOX
① 1

Record World
1

GOD SAVE US/
Do the Oz
BILL ELLIOTT/ELASTIC OZ BAND
(B-side: JOHN AND YOKO/ELASTIC OZ BAND)

Apple 1835
July 7, 1971 (July 5, 1971)

To assist the defendants in the famous *Oz* magazine obscenity trial in England, John wrote this pair of songs and rushed them out as a single in an effort to raise some defense money and public support.

The A-side, although sounding much like John, really featured Bill Elliott on lead vocal. Elliott later became one-half of the group Splinter, which recorded on George's Dark Horse label in the later seventies. The B-side was all-Lennon, with John and Yoko singing and squealing in front of a mass of noise.

Hardly anyone noticed or mentioned this undercover single by Lennon, and despite the A-side's being quite a good rocker, it soon vanished. Only *Record World* paid any attention to it.

CASH BOX

Record World

⊖

112

BANGLA-DESH/
Deep Blue
GEORGE HARRISON

Apple 1836
July 28, 1971

Three days before staging the historic "Concert for Bangla Desh," George rush released this single to help carry news to the outside world of the plight of the people of Bangla Desh. A most noble effort indeed, but on his third single out George failed to make the Top Ten for the first time, something which must have been especially painful, considering how sincere and hopeful he had been in trying to use his powerful influence over the record buyers and media of the Western World.

Radio airplay started out rather strong, but gradually fell off, and the single stalled out near the Top Twenty on two of the charts, though it almost made the Top Ten on *Record World*.

Billboard

23

CASH BOX

20

Record World

13

UNCLE ALBERT/ADMIRAL HALSEY//
Too Many People
PAUL AND LINDA McCARTNEY

Apple 1837
August 2, 1971 (August 9, 1971)

Paul's second solo single came from his second solo album, RAM, released a few months earlier. Rather than pick the single first, Paul waited to see which tunes were the most *wanted* by American radio stations and potential record buyers.

"Uncle Albert/Admiral Halsey" seemed the most likely choice for a pop hit, and it proved to be a correct one shooting rapidly up the charts and giving Paul his first solo Number One single.

Billboard
☆ 1

CASH BOX
① 1

Record World
1

IMAGINE/
It's So Hard
JOHN LENNON/PLASTIC ONO BAND

Apple 1840
October 11, 1971 (October 4, 1971)

A month after the release of the album *IMAGINE*, John issued the title track as a single. From the man who had proclaimed "the dream is over" came a beautiful and melodic statement from the dreamer, who painted a picture of what the perfect world could look like.

"Imagine" proved to be highly successful, giving John not only his biggest solo hit so far as a performer but also as a songwriter, for "Imagine" quickly became one of the most rerecorded songs ever written by Lennon or any of the Beatles. For much of the public and critics, this was quite possibly the most thoughtful and moving song John ever wrote. Though the charts were not quite so unanimous, this record clearly warranted the Number One status bestowed upon it by *Record World*.

Billboard	CASH BOX	Record World
☆ 3	②	1

72

HAPPY XMAS (War Is Over)/
Listen, the Snow Is Falling
JOHN AND YOKO/PLASTIC ONO BAND
(B-side: Yoko Ono/Plastic Ono Band)

Apple 1842
December 1, 1971 (December 6, 1971)

Following the Number One success of "Imagine," John envisioned topping the charts over the holidays with this special Christmas single, pressed in green vinyl no less, and complete with some excellent Phil Spector-produced special effects, such as sleigh bells and other assorted Christmas sounds. John and Yoko even revived their "War Is Over" slogan from 1969 and incorporated it into the lyrics.

As with most Christmas records, the single received only limited airplay. On the charts, it did fairly well on *Cash Box* and *Record World,* making the Top Forty, but on *Billboard* it became the very first Lennon single not to make the charts at all.

Billboard

☆
–

CASH BOX

（36）

Record World

28

GIVE IRELAND BACK TO THE IRISH/
(instrumental version)
WINGS

Apple 1847
February 28, 1972 (March 13, 1972)

The first official Wings single, this political statement from Paul caught everyone by surprise. Most people in America could not relate to its political commentary on events in Northern Ireland, and despite not being a half-bad rocker, neither the public nor the critics took to it with much enthusiasm.

Radio airplay was only marginal at best, while the chart action was mixed, with the record almost making the Top Twenty on *Billboard* but barely cracking the Top Forty on *Record World* and *Cash Box*.

21

CASH BOX

38

Record World

36

BACK OFF BOOGALOO
Blindman
RINGO STARR

Apple 1849
March 20, 1972 (April 3, 1972)

Ringo once again enlisted the aid of George as producer/guitarist and came up with another solid rocker. "Back Off Boogaloo" contained some of Ringo's strongest up-front drumming ever, while George's searing guitar wept throughout.

The single was a smash radio-play hit, and it firmly cemented Ringo's solo star status as not just a one-hit wonder. Certified Top Ten honors on all three charts.

Billboard

9

CASH BOX

10

Record World

8

WOMAN IS THE NIGGER OF THE WORLD/
Sisters O Sisters
JOHN LENNON/PLASTIC ONO BAND
(B-side: Yoko Ono/Plastic Ono Band)

Apple 1848
April 24, 1972 (May 8, 1972)

To say that this single raised a bit of a furor when it hit the streets is an understatement. For the second time in his career, John found his new record banned from the airwaves in most markets.

The song did not support or urge the use of the derogatory epithet for black people, but, rather, used "nigger" as a symbol for any and all oppressed people of the world, in this case women.

Nevertheless, much of the public began its outcry before waiting to hear the song or the accompanying explanation, and the fearful and concerned radio stations simply refused to play the record at all. Regardless of *that* word, it wasn't one of John's better songs anyway, and it soon became his least successful solo single, with *Billboard* and *Record World* disagreeing over how badly it placed, and *Cash Box* neglecting for the first time ever to chart a Lennon single.

Billboard

⭐ 57

CASH BOX

⊖

Record World

| 87 |

MARY HAD A LITTLE LAMB/LITTLE WOMAN LOVE
WINGS

Apple 1851
May 29, 1972 (June 5, 1972)

Mary Had A Little Lamb
1851

Little Woman Love
1851

Wings' second single seemed in direct opposition to the political atmosphere of their previous trip to the charts. However, this reworked nursery rhyme served only to create even more doubt in the public's and the critics' minds about Paul.

If taken for no more than it attempted to be, the tune was certainly an improvement over the traditional arrangement. Paul must have figured that this one was so simple that it was an obvious cinch to click. Unfortunately, that guess was wrong, and this single didn't sell very well or generate much airplay.

In an effort to try and insure some sort of hit, the flip side, "Little Woman Love," was pushed as well, with even a few of the picture sleeves having the flip-side title added to the back of the sleeve. And Apple even sent out promo copies with both sides appearing (rather than just the A-side as was usual) and a label stating the record to be by Paul McCartney *instead* of by Wings, obviously thinking that perhaps radio programmers did not realize that this record was by McCartney in the first place. It didn't help.

Billboard
28

CASH BOX
48

Record World
38

HI, HI, HI/
C Moon
WINGS

Apple 1857
December 4, 1972 (December 12, 1972)

Paul decided to set the record straight this time out with Wings, and prove that he and the band could indeed serve up some real rock 'n' roll. "Hi, Hi, Hi" was a most powerful rocker and it had knocked audiences dead along the "Wings Over Europe" tour during the summer of 1972.

The record gained a lot of airplay for Wings, and certainly helped Paul to recover from what had been a disastrous and shattering critical and public response for the past year and a half. The disc also returned Paul to the Top Ten, and was the start of one of the longest consecutive Top Ten hit streaks in the seventies by any artist.

Billboard
10

CASH BOX
6

Record World
7

MY LOVE/
  The Mess
PAUL McCARTNEY AND WINGS

Apple 1861
April 9, 1973 (April 16, 1973)

Paul seemed not the least bit shy about speaking of Linda's bedroom qualities in this slow romantic love ballad that served as a preview for the soon-to-follow RED ROSE SPEEDWAY album. As with "Hi, Hi, Hi," "My Love" was yet another song that had gone down quite well with European audiences the previous summer.

The record was a giant-sized hit, with radio airplay at saturation level in all markets, and it worked as a major factor in the complete 180-degree turnaround of Paul's popularity and critical standing from that of only one year previous.

This was Wings' second consecutive Top Ten score and Paul's second Number One solo single, and it served to spearhead an entire remainder-of-the-year outbreak of renewed Beatlemania and Beatles chart topping.

Billboard

☆ 1

CASH BOX

(1)

Record World

[1]

GIVE ME LOVE/
Miss O'Dell
GEORGE HARRISON

Apple 1862
May 7, 1973 (May 14, 1973)

George's first offering in almost two years was this very beautiful acoustic guitar ode to peace and love. The track was taken from his new album, LIVING IN THE MATERIAL WORLD.

It took off like a rocket and quickly followed McCartney's "My Love" to the top of the charts, eventually replacing it and giving the two ex-Beatles back-to-back Number One singles, a feat they duplicated on the album charts as well.

Radio airplay for this single was at the saturation level in most regions, and it would later prove to be George's second biggest solo success during the seventies, next only to "My Sweet Lord."

Billboard

1

CASH BOX

① 1

Record World

| 1 |

LIVE AND LET DIE/
I Lie Around
WINGS

Apple 1863
June 18, 1973

Paul observed his thirty-first birthday by releasing the title song he had written and performed for the new James Bond 007 motion picture, *Live and Let Die,* which provided another instant hit for the McCartney music machine. This George Martin produced single sped frighteningly fast right to the top of the charts, although its Number One glory was marred by *Billboard,* which stalled it at No. 2 for three weeks in a row, during which time both *Cash Box* and *Record World* placed it in the top spot on their charts.

"Live and Let Die" gave Paul his third solo Number One single, Wings their second consecutive Number One single, and the third straight Top Ten hit for the group.

2

CASH BOX

1

Record World

1

PHOTOGRAPH/
  Down and Out
RINGO STARR

Apple 1865
September 24, 1973 (October 1, 1973)

The first single issued from the RINGO album found Ringo teaming with fellow ex-Beatle George on a Starkey-Harrison composition featuring excellent production work by Richard Perry. This disc immediately received saturation-level airplay, and the Beatles-inspired record-buying public sent the sales figures soaring easily past the million mark.

No doubt about it this time around: the charts were unanimous in their acknowledgment of Number One rewards for Ringo. In addition to affording Ringo the experience of his biggest solo hit to date, this record also became the fourth consecutive single by an ex-Beatle to hit the top spot so far in 1973.

Billboard

☆ 1

CASH BOX

(1)

Record World

1

MIND GAMES/
Meat City
JOHN LENNON

Apple 1868
October 31, 1973 (October 22, 1973)

Paul, George, and Ringo had all scored Number One hit singles so far in 1973, and now it was John's turn. "Mind Games," his first release since the previous year's ill-fated "Woman Is the Nigger of the World," found John trying to return to and perhaps repeat the success of "Imagine."

Airplay was fairly heavy for this record, especially considering that there were at least three ex-Beatles singles vying for attention on the airwaves at the time. For many though, the magic needed to carry this over simply wasn't there, and the song finished short of the top spot, just barely hitting the Top Ten on only two of the three charts.

Billboard

18

CASH BOX

(10)

Record World

[10]

HELEN WHEELS/
Country Dreamer
PAUL McCARTNEY AND WINGS

Apple 1869
November 12, 1973 (November 5, 1973)

Paul and Wings' next single serving was a solid rocker, with lyrics based on their bus travels during the summer's tour of England and Scotland. The title came from the name of the Land-Rover Paul used on his farm in Scotland.

Although intended strictly as a non-album release, this track was added to the American version of the BAND ON THE RUN album at the last minute as an added sales booster. Wings gained their fourth straight Top Ten hit with this disc.

Billboard	CASH BOX	Record World
⭐10	⑤5	4

YOU'RE SIXTEEN/
  Devil Woman
RINGO STARR

Apple 1870
December 3, 1973

"You're Sixteen" was the second single lifted from the very successful RINGO album, and it boasts the assistance of Paul McCartney. Since all three fellow ex-Beatles helped out on the album, perhaps Ringo was trying to repay them by showcasing their individual appearances via his singles.

In any case, "You're Sixteen" became another major hit for Richard Starkey, M.B.E., going on to become not only one of the most heavily played singles over the holiday season but Ringo's second straight Number One single.

Billboard

CASH BOX

Record World

JET/Mamunia   (first issue)
JET/Let Me Roll It   (second issue)

PAUL McCARTNEY AND WINGS

Apple 1871
January 28, 1974 (first issue, subsequently deleted)
February 18, 1974 (second issue, replaced first)

Another smash-hit all-out rocker, "Jet" was the second single released from BAND ON THE RUN, which still had not sold as well as had been hoped. With the release of this single, the album stopped its holding pattern in the bottom half of the Top Ten and started its successful climb up the charts to Number One. "Jet" proved to be one of Paul's all-time most popular numbers, even scoring impressively with a lot of Wings' worst critics.

Capitol's initial choice for the B-side, "Mamunia," was shortly replaced by EMI's preference for the rest of the world, "Let Me Roll It."

Radio airplay was extremely heavy, though top honors went to Elton John and his similar-in-title-only "Bennie and the Jets" single, out at the same time. Just the same, Wings visited the Top Ten for the fifth time in a row.

Billboard

7

CASH BOX

5

Record World

5

OH MY MY/
Step Lightly
RINGO STARR

Apple 1872
February 18, 1974

"Oh My My" was chosen as the third and final single to be taken from the highly abundant RINGO album. A very rowdy piano stomper with heavy back-up vocals, this was yet another big hit for the former Beatle—who had to be surprising not only his three former counterparts but the entire music industry as well with his Midas-like touch for hit singles.

Heavy airplay and large sales from many new and younger fans unaware of the Beatles connection helped pave the way for this Top Ten disc.

Billboard

5

CASH BOX

6

Record World

5

BAND ON THE RUN/
Nineteen Hundred and Eighty Five
PAUL McCARTNEY AND WINGS

Apple 1873
April 8, 1974

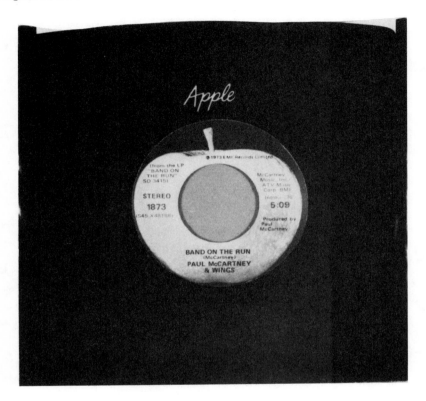

At long last, the title track of BAND ON THE RUN was released as a single. It soon proved to be the most successful of the album's three singles, not only going to the top of the charts itself but also helping to push the album back up to the top position on no fewer than two additional and separate occasions.

"Band on the Run," which changes total musical direction three times, was played at saturation level throughout much of the spring and summer, and was a solid and unanimous Number One hit for Paul and Wings.

Billboard CASH BOX *Record World*

1 1 1

88

WHATEVER GETS YOU THRU THE NIGHT/
Beef Jerky
JOHN LENNON

Apple 1874
September 23, 1974

Taken from his new album, WALLS AND BRIDGES, John's first new single in nearly a year was this almost unrecognizable high-energy pop duet sung with Elton John. (Many of the record reviews at the time noted that this record did not immediately sound like a John Lennon record. In fact, some reviewers went on to say that it could almost have been anybody.) The tune was certainly well-crafted and destined to become a major hit, owing to the three "C's" of pop music: catchy, commercial, and charming! "Whatever Gets You Thru the Night" was most certainly all three of those.

Radio response was the biggest for John since "Imagine," and this, coupled with very healthy sales, eventually raised the disc to the top of all three charts. Incredible as it may seem, this record gave Lennon only his very first Number One single on both *Billboard* and *Cash Box*, while only his second such chart topper on *Record World*.

Billboard

☆ 1

CASH BOX

① 1

Record World

| 1 |

JUNIOR'S FARM/SALLY G
PAUL McCARTNEY AND WINGS

Apple 1875
November 4, 1974 (November 11, 1974)

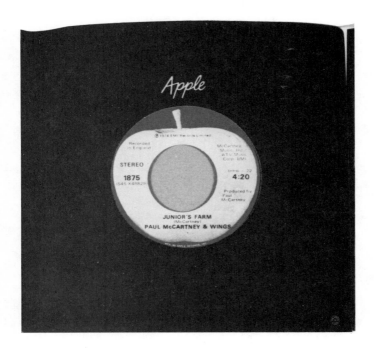

This single came as a result of Wings' visit to the city of Nashville in the summer of 1974. These two tracks would be the only new Wings material recorded in the country music capital ever to be heard outside Wings' studios and released to the public, except for a twin-instrumental single released under a pseudonym. In any case, "Junior's Farm" was yet another solid-thump-beat all-out rocker, while "Sally G" was a most engaging tribute to the country and western genre.

This single was definitely a double A-sided hit, though in most markets it was "Junior's Farm" that paced the way. During the record's last few weeks on the charts, "Sally G" took up the momentum, and was even charted as a separate entry by *Billboard,* climbing to No. 39 on its own after having peaked alongside "Junior's Farm" in the Top Five.

Billboard

☆ 3

CASH BOX

(4)

Record World

| 5 |

ONLY YOU/
Call Me
RINGO STARR

Apple 1876
November 11, 1974

The first single from Ringo's new GOODNIGHT VIENNA album was this highly unusual choice, a remake of the Platter's hit record from the fifties. Despite the odd selection, suggested by John Lennon, and Ringo's almost indistinguishable vocal, the disc clicked with both the radio stations and the record-buying public, perhaps due in part to some excellent and very catchy acoustic guitar playing by Dr. Winston O'Boogie, enabling the single to find its way to the Top Ten with no problem.

5

CASH BOX

6

Record World

9

DARK HORSE/
I Don't Care Anymore
GEORGE HARRISON

Apple 1877
November 18, 1974

George's first new vinyl product in a year and a half featured the title track of his new album, DARK HORSE, which also just happened to be the name of his new record company, as well as the name adopted for his first solo tour of the United States. "Dark Horse" was quickly recorded just before the start of the tour and featured a very hoarse-voiced Harrison, who had strained his vocal cords during rehearsals for the tour.

Reaction was mixed, though considering the fact that all four ex-Beatles had singles on the charts at the time, it still managed to gain a great deal of attention and airplay. The charts also seemed a bit uncertain about "Dark Horse," though it did make the Top Twenty on two of the three.

Billboard

☆ 15

CASH BOX

 19

Record World

27

WALKING IN THE PARK WITH ELOISE/
Bridge over the River Suite
THE COUNTRY HAMS

EMI 3977
December 2, 1974 (November 25, 1974)

The Country Hams were really Wings in disguise, and this pair of harmless instrumentals were the only other tracks recorded in Nashville besides "Junior's Farm"/"Sally G" ever to be heard by the public.

The A-side was a tune written many years past by Paul's father, and, like the flip side, was pleasant enough, but certainly of no commercial potential in the current pop music arena. As such, this record didn't catch anybody's attention, save for a few McCartney collectors who were lucky enough even to find this very uncirculated piece of wax. More of a McCartney family project and Paul's personal tribute to his father than anything else (which was at least a most noble gift) there was no radio airplay or chart action.

Billboard

CASH BOX

Record World

#9 DREAM/
What You Got
JOHN LENNON

Apple 1878
December 16, 1974

The second single to be pulled from WALLS AND BRIDGES was this lush and dreamy ballad. "#9 Dream" was a soft and flowing piece of dream-inspired seduction. Initially Apple had hoped to make this record a double-sided hit, and so issued separate promo discs for the B-side, "What You Got," in an unsuccessful attempt to get the disco and soul audiences interested.

"#9 Dream" was the definite hit, and radio airplay was strong in many markets, with the single eventually finding its way into the Top Ten on two of the three charts, while cosmically clocking in precisely at the Number Nine position on *Billboard!*

9

CASH BOX

10

Record World

17

DING DONG; DING DONG/
  Hari's On Tour (Express)
GEORGE HARRISON

Apple 1879
December 23, 1974

The second single from the DARK HORSE album, this "Happy New Year" anthem was released just too close to the actual holiday to stand even a hair of a chance of gaining much radio airplay or store sales before the holidays had passed and everybody had moved on to new business.

While many critics killed this song, and especially the lyrics, it was really done in good nature and merely served up as an alternative to traditional holiday song fare. Nevertheless, it was only about half as successful as the previous "Dark Horse" single, both in terms of radio reaction and chart placement.

36

CASH BOX

36

Record World

49

NO NO SONG/SNOOKEROO
RINGO STARR

Apple 1880
January 27, 1975

The follow-up single plucked from GOODNIGHT VIENNA was the Hoyt Axton novelty, "No No Song," backed by Elton John's "Snookeroo," which became a double A-sided hit in many markets. "No No Song" could hardly have been called a serious threat, but it was all for fun and easily identifiable with not only Ringo's personable character, but perhaps his well-publicized excursions at the bar and backroom as well.

A very large amount of radio airplay helped to push this record to the top of one chart, and almost to the top of the other two.

3

CASH BOX

1

Record World

3

STAND BY ME/
  Move Over Ms. L
JOHN LENNON

Apple 1881
March 10, 1975

Almost a month after the ROCK 'N' ROLL album had been rush released, Apple finally pulled the first single from Lennon's oldies collection. "Stand By Me" was given the nod, but despite a fairly good start gradually stalled out just as it reached the Top Twenty. It just might have been the lack of excitement and spark that finally caused the radio audience and record-buying public to grow tired of it long before expected, regardless of Lennon's fine vocal and the excellent and faithful production.

Billboard

⭐ 20

CASH BOX

(20)

Record World

[24]

LISTEN TO WHAT THE MAN SAID/
Love in Song
WINGS

Capitol 4091
May 23, 1975 (May 19, 1975)

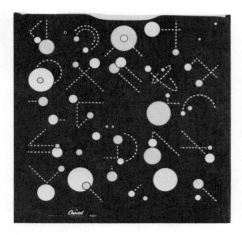

Wings' first single in several months was this initial pick from the soon-to-follow VENUS AND MARS album. The tune flows right along and much better than might be expected, given its somewhat awkward title. This was one of several McCartney singles over the years that didn't hook you at first listen but instead grew on you the more you heard it.

Nevertheless, the song became very popular, and the eventual saturation level of radio airplay carried on for most of the summer. Yet another Number One success for Wings, and their eighth consecutive trip to the Top Ten.

Billboard

1

CASH BOX

1

Record World

1

IT'S ALL DOWN TO GOODNIGHT VIENNA/OO-WEE
RINGO STARR

Apple 1882
June 2, 1975

Finally, Dr. Winston O'Boogie managed to get Ringo to issue a Lennon composition on the A-side of the new Starr single. Yet strangely, this was by far and away the least successful of the six singles issued from the RINGO and GOODNIGHT VIENNA albums. By rights, this should have been one of the most prosperous. "Goodnight Vienna" was re-edited so as to include the reprise from side two of the album, which, in effect, created a brand new full-length version of the song. "Oo-Wee" was also a hit in many markets, making this another double A-sided release.

Even so, neither gained a lot of airplay; perhaps the fact that the album was now some eight months old had something to do with both songs' failure to stir much excitement at this point. Although unknown at the time, this was an omen that Ringo's King Midas touch for hit singles was suddenly to disappear.

Billboard

⭐ 31

CASH BOX

(29)

Record World

| 54 |

SLIPPIN' AND SLIDIN'/AIN'T THAT A SHAME
JOHN LENNON

Apple 1883
(June 2, 1975—unreleased)

This was to have been the second single from John's ROCK 'N' ROLL album. Promotional copies were sent out for each side of this disc in an attempt to make certain it would be a double A-sided hit. But at the last minute, despite a well-timed promotional appearance on U.S. television by Lennon, singing "Slippin' and Slidin' " on ABC-TV's *Salute to Sir Lew Grade* special, the single was held back from release.

Pulling this disc from release was even more odd because many radio stations had already picked up on the record and were beginning to add it to their playlists. Oh well, ain't that a shame.

YOU/
  World of Stone
GEORGE HARRISON

Apple 1884
September 15, 1975

After seemingly going into hiding following the DARK HORSE album and tour, George emerged in the early fall of 1975 with this single as a preview of his new EXTRA TEXTURE album. In truth, this track was really an outtake, left over from the 1970 ALL THINGS MUST PASS sessions, and George simply added a new vocal recording over the instrumental track. Unfortunately, although George's voice had recovered from its excessive hoarseness, it no longer was strong enough to carry certain notes, and, particularly in this song, his singing simply sounded too weak to be fully effective.

Radio reaction was fair to good, depending on the market, and the song was popular enough to put George back into the Top Twenty on all but *Record World*.

Billboard

20

CASH BOX

19

Record World

39

LETTING GO/
You Gave Me the Answer
WINGS

Capitol 4145
September 29, 1975 (September 22, 1975)

"Letting Go" was the second single from VENUS AND MARS. Perhaps fearing that this slightly laid-back rocker was a bit too laid-back, the single version was remixed and was much *hotter* than its album counterpart.

While later proving to be an enormous concert favorite for Wings, the record failed to click on the American scene, and not only broke Wings' streak of Top Ten hits, but was Wings' worst outing on the charts up to this point. A real shame, as it was a good track and deserved better reaction.

Billboard

39

CASH BOX

41

Record World

62

VENUS AND MARS/ROCK SHOW//
Magneto and Titanium Man
WINGS

Capitol 4175
October 27, 1975 (November 3, 1975)

Because of the unexpected failure of "Letting Go," this third single from VENUS AND MARS was rush released so quickly that both singles were on the charts simultaneously for a time.

"Venus and Mars/Rock Show" was constructed in much the same highly successful manner that the singles "Uncle Albert/Admiral Halsey" and "Band on the Run" had been; that is, each track was really a combination of several song fragments segued to produce a single tune that changed musical direction several times throughout. However, the results this time out were not as triumphant—hard to figure, since "Venus and Mars" was quite pretty, and "Rock Show" was a magnificent rocker in true Madison Square Garden spirit.

Airplay was only fair to good in most markets, though it did score far better in the charts than the previous single. Still, while coming somewhat close on at least two of the charts, Wings suddenly experienced their second single in a row that failed to make the Top Ten.

Billboard

12

CASH BOX

16

Record World

28

THIS GUITAR/
Maya Love
GEORGE HARRISON

Apple 1885
December 8, 1975

EXTRA TEXTURE's second single would soon prove to be the very last Apple Records single ever released, the first ex-Beatle single to contain a song from a previous album ("Maya Love" was from DARK HORSE), and the first single for George that failed to make the charts at all.

"This Guitar," the sequel to "While My Guitar Gently Weeps," didn't contain enough of a solid bite for most of the public, and the disc failed to generate any radio airplay or activity at the cash register. A sad end for the Apple era.

Billboard

CASH BOX

Record World

SILLY LOVE SONGS/
Cook of the House
WINGS

Capitol 4256
April 1, 1976 (April 12, 1976)

One of the most-loved and most-hated McCartney songs of all time, this single served up Paul's biggest Number One success since "My Love." The success of "Silly Love Songs" was helped in part by Wings' touring of the States for the first time ever, and by Paul's appearing before live American audiences for the first time in nearly a decade.

This single, pulled from WINGS AT THE SPEED OF SOUND, reached even new levels of saturation airplay for the former Beatle. An easy choice for top honors on all three American record charts.

CASH BOX

(1)

Record World

1

1

GOT TO GET YOU INTO MY LIFE/
Helter Skelter
THE BEATLES

Capitol 4274
May 31, 1976

Capitol's first Beatles single in six years was launched in an effort to cash in on the fact that McCartney was on tour in the United States. And, since he was very much the lead vocal on this track, it certainly couldn't hurt in pushing Capitol's new ROCK 'N' ROLL MUSIC repackage album.

Interestingly, the B-side, "Helter Skelter," was originally going to be the A-side, as the result of a television movie dealing with the famed Manson family murders (which supposedly were inspired in part by the family's erroneous interpretation of the song's lyrics). In fact, promotional singles of "Helter Skelter" were sent out to radio stations. However, by the time the record was ready, it was decided to opt for the more potentially commercial "Got to Get You into My Life," and the choice proved to be a good one.

This Beatles single-that-never-was did extremely well, especially considering its ten-year age. Radio airplay was at heavy to near-saturation levels in most markets, and this was one of the most-heard songs of the summer. The charts disagreed slightly as to just how popular it really was.

CASH BOX

Record World

Billboard ☆ 7

③ 3

9

LET 'EM IN/
Beware My Love
WINGS

Capitol 4293
June 28, 1976

Taking full advantage of their cross-country American tour, which had just scored a whopping success, Wings rushed out the second SPEED OF SOUND single even as "Silly Love Songs" remained near the top of the charts.

Another soft-pop tune, the almost sluggish pace of "Let 'Em In" seemed to grow gradually on everyone until it became an unqualified smash hit. It gained extensive radio coverage for the remainder of the summer although the charts seemed a bit unsure of just how massive a hit it really was, with only *Cash Box* slipping it into the Number One slot.

Billboard

★ 3

CASH BOX

(1)

Record World

4

A DOSE OF ROCK 'N' ROLL/
Cryin'
RINGO STARR

Atlantic 3361
September 20, 1976

This was Ringo's first new recording in almost two years, and also the first single to be lifted from his first Atlantic album, RINGO'S ROTOGRAVURE.

This fifties-flavored jingle plodded along and failed to stir much excitement or long-term interest. With the help of some fair radio airplay, especially upon release, it eventually slipped into the Top Thirty, or thereabouts.

Billboard 26

CASH BOX 26

Record World 32

OB-LA-DI OB-LA-DA/
Julia
THE BEATLES

Capitol 4347
November 8, 1976 (November 1, 1976)

Capitol tried to keep the summer's Beatles/Wings-mania going until Christmas with the release of this record, another McCartney-sung single-that-never-was, this time taken from THE BEATLES ("White Album").

However, this record came so late in the year that much of the Beatles/Wings-mania of the summer had already died down. Despite the very clever use of a picture sleeve similar in design to the cover of the THE BEATLES ("White Album"), complete with individual number stamping, this record simply failed to gain any real momentum. Record sales not only lagged, but radio programmers were more concerned with songs less than eight years old.

Billboard

CASH BOX

Record World

| 75 |

THIS SONG/
Learning How to Love You
GEORGE HARRISON

Dark Horse DRC 8294
November 15, 1976

This single—the first from THIRTY THREE & ⅓—was written as a statement on the recent lawsuit decision against George for supposedly plagiarizing in "My Sweet Lord" the Chiffon's "He's So Fine."

In spite of the abundance of news coverage concerning the trial, the tongue-in-cheek humor of the lyrics, and one of George's most uplifting and inspired musical tunes in years, this single somehow managed not to sell half as well as had been hoped or expected. Climbing right up the charts, it suddenly stopped one day, and soon fell off for no apparent rhyme or reason. Radio airplay had been fairly good, but as the holidays approached, some unexplainable force overcame its progress and pulled the rug out.

Billboard

☆ 25

CASH BOX

(28)

Record World

[33]

HEY BABY/
Lady Gaye
RINGO STARR

Atlantic 3371
November 22, 1976

"Hey Baby" was the second single from RINGO'S ROTOGRAVURE. This heavy-background-chorus-sung shuffle more or less got lost in the shuffle. Virtually no airplay on the radio at all resulted in the least successful of all the ex-Beatles singles out at the time.

Although released in late November, it would not even chart until the end of February, and would go down as the final chart appearance inside the Top 100 for Ringo during the seventies. The charts differed only in how poorly this single scored.

Billboard	CASH BOX	Record World
74	(62)	93

CRACKERBOX PALACE/
Learning How to Love You
GEORGE HARRISON

Dark Horse DRC 8313
January 24, 1977

The second single from THIRTY THREE & ⅓ was the album track that had received the most airplay and critical praise. "Crackerbox Palace" proved to be much more popular than its predecessor, "This Song." In fact, it did quite well, receiving a great deal of airplay, and for a time even managed to pace ahead of McCartney's "Maybe I'm Amazed" single.

The record contained the same B-side as "This Song," and the only explanation ever hinted at was George's mentioning in an interview that he felt "Learning How to Love You" was his most beautiful love song since "Something": perhaps he felt it deserved more recognition than it had gotten.

Billboard   **CASH BOX**   **Record World**

19   17   26

MAYBE I'M AMAZED/
Soily
WINGS

Capitol 4385
February 7, 1977

Almost two months after the release of the WINGS OVER AMERICA album, this single was finally pulled and issued. "Maybe I'm Amazed" was the single-that-never-was from the original McCARTNEY debut solo album, and this live version was served up to correct that situation once and for all.

Radio airplay was fairly good, but sales could have been much better. Perhaps most already owned McCARTNEY or WINGS OVER AMERICA or both. Nonetheless, the single managed to get just into the Top Ten on two of the three charts, with only *Record World* disagreeing by a wide margin.

Billboard

10

CASH BOX
10

Record World
26

SEASIDE WOMAN/
B-Side to Seaside
SUZY AND THE RED STRIPES

Epic 8-50403
May 31, 1977

Another Wings-in-disguise effort, Linda McCartney's long-awaited "Seaside Woman" was finally released in 1977. Reportedly recorded in 1971, and performed live during Wings' tours of 1972 and 1973, this disc was issued on the Epic label because of the McCartney clan's contractual obligations with EMI/Capitol.

Despite its reggae flavor and release during a period when reggae-inspired music was popular with the public, this record was treated more as a novelty item and not given any serious airplay or critical consideration, all of which was reflected by the charts.

Billboard

59

CASH BOX

58

Record World

92

WINGS/
    Just a Dream
RINGO STARR

Atlantic 3429
August 25, 1977

This record came about as the result of a last-minute switch, being selected instead of "Drowning in the Sea of Love" as the first U.S. single to be taken from the new RINGO THE 4th album.

Never mind the alluring title, the song had nothing at all to do with Paul's solo group, and, likewise, the record-buying public, critics, and radio stations had nothing at all to do with this disc. It bombed completely, giving Ringo his first solo single not to make the Top 100 on the U.S. singles charts, although *Record World* placed it as high as No. 119 on its list of records bubbling under the Top 100.

CASH BOX

Record World

119

DROWNING IN THE SEA OF LOVE/
Just a Dream
RINGO STARR

Atlantic 3412
October 18, 1977

This rather than "Wings" was supposed to have been the initial single released from the RINGO THE 4th album, as can be noted by this disc's lower catalog number. For some reason, it was held back at the last minute and "Wings" went out instead. When it became obvious that "Wings" had failed, this record was hurriedly shipped out, sporting the same B-side.

Radio response was nil even though Atlantic issued a special twelve-inch promo copy of the single to radio stations. This time, Ringo failed even to bubble under the Top 100 on any of the charts. Drowning was right.

CASH BOX

Record World

MULL OF KINTYRE/GIRL'S SCHOOL
WINGS

Capitol 4504
November 14, 1977

Recognizing that 1977 had not been an especially good year on the charts for McCartney—or for any of the ex-Beatles for that matter—Paul decided to change that by making his new single a double A-sided hit, hoping to please both soft-pop and hard-rock fans in one shot.

While the rest of the Free World went crazy over the Scottish-flavored ballad, "Mull of Kintyre," the U.S. radio stations ignored it completely. Instead, they opted for the flip side, another patented McCartney rocker, "Girl's School," which also had been doing quite well overseas. Unfortunately, between the still-strong disco fad and the upsurging punk rock mood at the time, neither side of this single really managed to click for Paul in the States. "Girl's School" eventually closed in on the Top Thirty, then quickly disappeared, while Capitol mulled over why "Mull of Kintyre" had not gone anywhere.

Billboard

☆ 33

CASH BOX

(31)

Record World

33

GIRL/
You're Gonna Lose That Girl
THE BEATLES

Capitol 4506
(November 1977—unreleased)

This single, pulled from the LOVE SONGS repackage album, was never released. Promotional copies were sent out to radio stations, and the single was added to playlists and began receiving airplay in a number of markets. However, the record was held back at the last moment. A couple of possible reasons have been mentioned as to why this occurred.

First, LOVE SONGS was not selling as well as had been hoped for, and perhaps this wasn't the strongest choice for that all-important single needed to help boost sales.

Perhaps more credible though was word that Capitol held back this release so as not to compete with Wings' "Girl's School" single, which simply wasn't selling either. Reportedly, Capitol also felt that it would be detrimental to have two singles out simultaneously with a total of three tracks between them sharing the word *girl* in the title, thus potentially creating confusion for many record buyers. Whatever the reasons, the fact remains that despite radio airplay this single was never officially released.

WITH A LITTLE LUCK//
Backwards Traveler/Cuff-Link
WINGS

Capitol 4559
March 20, 1978

The first single from Wings' album LONDON TOWN, this seemingly lightweight bit of pop music was another of the many McCartney singles that at first didn't impress many, but tended to grow on everyone until it gained momentum and became a massive hit. A very oddly paced tune, it was nonetheless a fine bit of musicianship.

A major radio airplay success, this song returned Paul and Wings to the top of the charts, and served to ease somewhat the still-lingering wounds suffered from the failure of "Girl's School"/"Mull of Kintyre" in the States.

1

CASH BOX

1

Record World

1

LIPSTICK TRACES/
Old Time Relovin'
RINGO STARR

Portrait 6-70015
April 18, 1978

This harmless tune was served up as the first single to be extracted from the BAD BOY album. Although Ringo had shifted to the Portrait label, his bad luck streak remained unchanged, with "Lipstick Traces" soon suffering the identical fate of his last two 45rpm outings for Atlantic—giving the ex-Beatle his third single in a row failing to place inside the Top 100. Only *Record World* bothered with it, placing the disc just out of Top 100 reach at No. 103.

Billboard

☆

CASH BOX

⊖

Record World

103

I'VE HAD ENOUGH/
Deliver Your Children
WINGS

Capitol 4594
June 12, 1978

This was the second single from LONDON TOWN. An all-out McCartney rocker, complete with fifties-style spoken lyrics in the middle of the number, Paul delivered it with a slight Elvis impersonation.

The song ignited a very large amount of airplay, and based on that alone certainly should have made it an easy Top Ten hit. Apparently sales lagged, as this single ran out of steam just after making the Top Thirty.

Billboard 25

CASH BOX (28)

Record World 30

HEART ON MY SLEEVE/
Who Needs a Heart
RINGO STARR

Portrait 6-70018
July 6, 1978

Released after BAD BOY had already failed on the album charts, this second single from that album was quietly slipped out. Portrait seemingly did little promotion for the record, and despite its being a very good song selection for Ringo the disc died a quiet and unnoticed death.

This would prove to be Ringo's last single released during the seventies, and certainly a sad note on which to end the decade. After having so easily topped the charts during the first half of the seventies, Ringo consistently failed even to make the charts in the second half. Perhaps partly to blame was the choice of inferior material, and partly an ever-changing record-buying public, which by the late seventies was either into disco or punk. Ringo found himself unable to gain acceptance from these crowds, and seemed to alienate his former pop-rock fans as well.

SGT. PEPPER'S LONELY HEARTS CLUB BAND/WITH A LITTLE HELP FROM MY FRIENDS//
A Day in the Life
THE BEATLES

Capitol 4612
August 14, 1978

With the release of the *Sgt. Pepper's Lonely Hearts Club Band* motion picture during the summer of 1978 came a much renewed interest in the Beatles original album from 1967. Capitol remixed and reissued the album, including a picture disc version, and it did quite well in gaining many new sales, mostly from fans who were hearing the group for the first time.

In a similar vein, Capitol rushed out this single to compete with a similar single from the film's soundtrack by Peter Frampton and the Bee Gees, although it soon became apparent that those concerned enough with the original versions by the Beatles were choosing to buy the entire album, and for the most part were ignoring this single. Radio airplay was fair at first, then dropped off suddenly and completely. The charts disagreed only over how big of a flop it was.

71

CASH BOX

92

Record World

103

LONDON TOWN/
  I'm Carrying
WINGS

Capitol 4625
August 21, 1978

The third and final single from LONDON TOWN was the title track. A pleasant if somewhat sluggish exercise in mellow English pop, this single just didn't have enough charisma to gain it much in the way of sales or airplay. The album was already slipping down the charts by the time this was issued, and the disc received very little exposure on the airwaves.

Noted mainly at the time for sharing honors with "Letting Go" as Wings' least successful chart single up to that point, it would prove to be McCartney's last single for Capitol Records.

Billboard

39

CASH BOX

42

Record World

48

BLOW AWAY/
Soft Hearted Hana
GEORGE HARRISON

Dark Horse DRC 8763
February 14, 1979

After a customary two-year absence, George returned in early 1979 with one of his most uplifting, cheerful, and commercial tunes in many a record. "Blow Away," the first single from his new GEORGE HARRISON album, received a great deal of airplay, returning George to the radio waves of America, and giving him his biggest chart success, up to this point, since 1973's "Give Me Love"—although still falling short of the Top Ten.

Billboard

16

CASH BOX

12

Record World

17

125

GOODNIGHT TONIGHT/
Daytime Nightime Suffering
WINGS

Columbia 3-10939
Columbia 23-10940 (special 12-inch long version disco single)
March 15, 1979

With McCartney's first offering on his new label, Columbia, Wings ventured into disco music, a move which proved to be an interesting one, to say the least, and immediately drew the largest amount of anti-McCartney criticism in a number of years.

The record wasn't given all that much airplay, even on the many all-disco stations that flourished at the time, but apparently it sold well enough to result in yet another Top Ten hit for Wings. A special long version of the song was issued on a twelve-inch disco single.

Billboard

5

CASH BOX

4

Record World

7

GETTING CLOSER/
Spin It On
WINGS

Columbia 3-11020
June 5, 1979

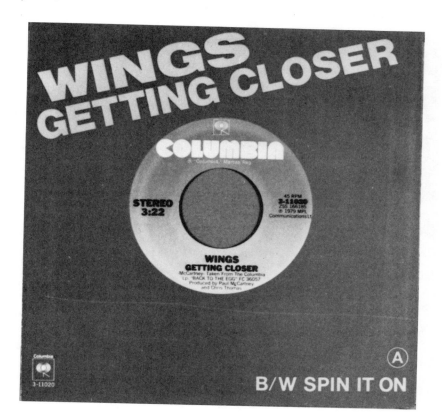

Wings' second Columbia single was also the first drafted from their debut Columbia album, BACK TO THE EGG. "Getting Closer" was still another in the long string of all-out basic rockers over the years from Paul, this time perhaps hoping to recapture many of his fans turned off by the previous disco single.

"Getting Closer" received a good deal of airplay but was unable to produce enough chart action to take it inside the Top Twenty.

  CASH BOX   *Record World*

20   20   22

127

LOVE COMES TO EVERYONE/
Soft Touch
GEORGE HARRISON

Dark Horse DRC 8844
May 9, 1979

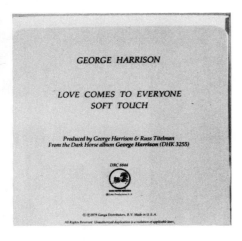

When the GEORGE HARRISON album was released, this had been one of the tracks getting most of the airplay. However, when it was issued as the second single from the album, it quickly died. Radio airplay dropped to practically zero. Sales were so poor that even before the record's picture sleeve could be sent out, the initial shipment of records was already being returned from the stores, and the sleeve was withdrawn.

Only *Record World* placed it on their list of records waiting to enter the Top 100, something it never went on to accomplish.

Billboard

CASH BOX

⊖

Record World

| 118 |

128

ARROW THROUGH ME/
Old Siam, Sir
WINGS

Columbia 1-11070
August 14, 1979

All right, since the rocker didn't do it, back to a soft-pop tune; "Arrow Through Me" was selected as the next single from BACK TO THE EGG. Evidently the song seemed a bit too conducive to sleep to stir much radio activity, which was only marginally fair at best.

It's hard to believe that this disc did almost as well on the charts as "I've Had Enough," and better overall than "Girl's School," but such was the music business's and record-buying public's unpredictable taste in the late seventies.

CASH BOX

Record World

28

36

27

WONDERFUL CHRISTMASTIME/
Rudolph the Red-Nosed Reggae
PAUL McCARTNEY

Columbia 1-11162
November 20, 1979

Alas, another ex-Beatle Christmas record. George had blessed the 1970 holiday season with "My Sweet Lord," John had followed in 1971 with "Happy Xmas," and so, some eight years later, Paul apparently decided it was his turn to issue a surefire homespun Christmas carol, certain to become an all-time classic of its own.

Unfortunately, "Wonderful Christmastime" failed to impress anyone in the States. The radio stations and the record charts all ignored it, as did most of the record-buying public. The critics all but thought the disc was some sort of joke (although Paul was indeed serious). Most of the attention at the time went to the fact that the record was credited simply to Paul McCartney (without Wings), making for his first truly solo single in eight years.

Even though the disc made the Top Ten in England, it failed to make any of the three American charts, giving Paul his first total chart failure.

Billboard

CASH BOX

Record World

Coming Up//COMING UP (live version)
  Lunch Box Odd Sox
PAUL McCARTNEY
  (B-side: PAUL McCARTNEY AND WINGS)

Columbia 1-11263
April 15, 1980

As a preview to the upcoming McCARTNEY II solo album, Paul released his second single in a row without Wings—sort of. "Coming Up" was meant to be the new Paul McCartney single, and as a bonus, the flip side included a live version of the song, recorded during Wings' 1979 UK tour. However, the speeded-up vocals on the studio version did little to thrill American radio programmers, so they flipped the record over and played the much stronger, normal-McCartney-voiced live version by Paul and Wings.

The live single became the smash hit, and returned Paul to the top of the charts, or at least close enough for comfort, as this record enjoyed enormous popularity and received saturation-level airplay.

Billboard

CASH BOX

(2)

Record World

3

WATERFALLS/
Check My Machine
PAUL McCARTNEY

Columbia 1-11335
July 22, 1980

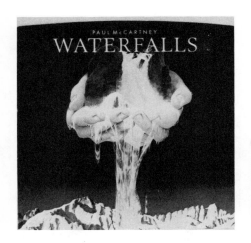

"Waterfalls" was the second single from McCARTNEY II, a slow-moving ballad that, according to Paul, was the one song that everybody who heard the album kept insisting should be the next single.

With American radio tastes suddenly shifting back to a somewhat harder sound, this choice proved to be just too tame, and the record received very little airplay. It not only failed to help revive the slowing sales of the album, but it also failed to raise any sales of its own, resulting in Paul's all-time second-worst showing on the American charts.

Billboard

106

CASH BOX

—

Record World

83

(JUST LIKE) STARTING OVER/
Kiss Kiss Kiss
JOHN LENNON
(B-side: Yoko Ono)

Geffen GEF-49604
October 23, 1980

After a seemingly endless five-year absence from the music scene, John returned with renewed enthusiasm and vitality, and released the fifties-flavored "(Just Like) Starting Over," one of Lennon's most catchy, endearing, and commercial tunes ever, reminiscent at times of the early Beatles sound. For John, his career, his outlook on life—in fact, his whole mental attitude—was indeed one of starting over. For the fans, this was certainly worth the wait.

Amid much publicity of John's reemergence, the single quickly took off, ripping up the charts and gaining a very heavy amount of radio airplay. It was already in the Top Five and steadily climbing toward the top when tragedy struck. In the week that followed, "Starting Over" suddenly took on an even deeper meaning. For some, it seemed so ironic. For many others, the richness of Lennon's lyrics and tone of voice served only to give hope of better things to come. Needless to say, the single immediately ascended to the Number One position on all three charts, staying there for several weeks in early 1981.

Billboard

1

CASH BOX

1

Record World

1

WOMAN/
  Beautiful Boys
JOHN LENNON
  (B-side: Yoko Ono)

Geffen 49644
January 12, 1981 (January 9, 1981)

The second single to be issued from DOUBLE FANTASY was this extremely beautiful love ballad from John to Yoko. This very appealing ode was called "the Beatle track" by John, and it was clearly one of the high points on the album. Indeed, to many it did in fact sound like Beatle John, and as a result, the single raced up the charts and gained saturation-level airplay everywhere. Once it entered the Top Ten it remained there for more than two months, although only *Cash Box* raised it to the coveted Number One position, while both *Billboard* and *Record World* let it hold at No. 2 for several weeks. Nevertheless, thanks to *Cash Box*, John Lennon had his second Number One in a row from DOUBLE FANTASY.

Billboard

☆ 2

CASH BOX

① 1

Record World

2

134

WATCHING THE WHEELS/
   Yes I'm Your Angel
JOHN LENNON
   (B-side: Yoko Ono)

Geffen 49695
March 13, 1981

"Watching the Wheels" became the third single released off DOUBLE FANTASY. This piano-driven "Imagine"-like tune was John's personal answer to all those who questioned his five-year "retirement." Upon the album's release, this track was singled out as one of John's best. However, in the wake of his tragic death what had seemed beautiful suddenly turned quite haunting as well.

Still, despite the fact that several million copies of DOUBLE FANTASY had already been sold, this single managed to perform superbly. Radio airplay was at saturation level, while on the charts John managed his third Top Ten single in a row.

    CASH BOX   *Record World*

10   7   9

ALL THOSE YEARS AGO/
Writing's on the Wall
GEORGE HARRISON

Dark Horse DRC 49725
May 11, 1981 (May 7, 1981)

The highly publicized John Lennon tribute song by the three surviving Beatles originally was written by George for Ringo's CAN'T FIGHT LIGHTNING album, and was recorded with both George and Ringo playing on the track during that album's mid-1980 sessions (with different lyrics). However, Ringo decided against using it, and left it off the album.

Following John's murder, George decided to put new lyrics to the music and include it on his own SOMEWHERE IN ENGLAND album, which he happened to be rerecording at the time. Paul and Linda McCartney dropped by Harrison's home studio and added backing vocals. The result was a track featuring George, Ringo, and Paul.

With this revelation accompanying the release of the single, the disc quickly shot up the charts as radio programmers around the world were swift to add what many termed the new "Beatles reunion/Lennon tribute" number to their playlists. On the charts, the record just missed the top spot, but provided George with his first Top Ten hit since "Give Me Love" all those years ago in 1973.

Billboard

CASH BOX

③

Record World

TEARDROPS/
Save the World
GEORGE HARRISON

Dark Horse DRC 79825
July 24, 1981 (July 15, 1981)

When "Teardrops" was released as the second single from SOMEWHERE IN ENGLAND, all three trade publications earmarked the bouncy, almost Elton John-like disc to repeat the Top Five success of George's previous outing.

However, the majority of the nation's radio programmers disagreed, and the result was virtually no airplay. This, coupled with dismal sales, was clearly reflected by the lackluster chart action for this certainly more-deserving single.

CASH BOX

Record World

WRACK MY BRAIN/
Drumming Is My Madness
RINGO STARR

Boardwalk NB7-11-130
October 27, 1981 (October 23, 1981)

Ringo returned to the world of pop music with this George Harrison written and produced number as his first record release in more than three years—and his first for yet another label—Boardwalk.

"Wrack My Brain" was an enjoyable exercise in pop music, with excellent production as always by fellow ex-Beatle George. And upon closer examination, the lyrics, while applying just as aptly to Ringo's state of affairs, were clearly motivated by George's own experiences and could have easily been a welcome addition to Harrison's own SOMEWHERE IN ENGLAND.

Nonetheless, "Wrack My Brain" proved a suitable choice for Ringo's reentry, gaining him a fair amount of airplay (although given the makeup of the playlist fare at the time, certainly deserved more exposure than it got) as well as enough supporting sales to reward him with his first Top Forty hit in five years.

38

CASH BOX

37

Record World

40

PRIVATE PROPERTY/
Stop and Take the Time to Smell the Roses
RINGO STARR

Boardwalk NB7-11-134
January 13, 1982

The follow-up single chosen for release from STOP AND SMELL THE ROSES was "Private Property," a tune written and produced by McCartney, which along with Harrison's "Wrack My Brain" was regarded by many critics as among the better numbers on the album.

Unfortunately, radio station personnel and the general public knew better than to dare touch an item marked "Private Property," and as a result, this single suffered an unfair case of severe neglect, as it failed to generate any airplay or sales.

139

THE BEATLES MOVIE MEDLEY/
Fab Four on Film
THE BEATLES

Capitol B-5100
(March 15, 1982—unreleased)

THE BEATLES MOVIE MEDLEY/
I'm Happy Just to Dance with You
THE BEATLES

Capitol B-5107
March 22, 1982

THE BEATLES MOVIE MEDLEY contains excerpts of the songs: Magical Mystery Tour / All You Need Is Love / You've Got to Hide Your Love Away / I Should Have Known Better / A Hard Day's Night / Ticket to Ride / Get Back

This record surfaced almost a full year after a pair of imitation-Beatles medley singles had appeared (the initial "Stars On" tribute topped the charts in 1981; the follow-up fizzled). Nonetheless, Capitol saw fit to splice together excerpts from seven of the group's motion picture tunes in order to create the first *new* Beatles single in more than three years. Surprisingly, though, in spite of the fact that many of the shifts between songs were rather abrupt and amateurishly edited, and the fact that some of the songs were actually sped-up electronically, the general public's apparent hunger for *any* Beatles' product more than a dozen years after the break-up could be evidenced by this near-atrocity almost cracking the Top Ten, in addition to garnering fairly good radio airplay in most markets.

The original B-side was to have featured an interview recorded during the filming of *A Hard Day's Night,* but due to reported legal difficulties was substituted just prior to release with the track "I'm Happy Just to Dance With You." This change was made after Capitol had already sent out promotional copies of the B-5100 disc and picture sleeve. Commercial copies of B-5100 awaiting shipment were immediately withdrawn and reportedly scrapped. The new B-5107 disc (and revised picture sleeve) was quickly rushed out in its place, although the release was delayed a week.

Billboard

CASH BOX
14

Record World
39*

After debuting at No. 64, the record jumped to No. 39 for the week of 4/10/82, after which Record World ceased publication.

EBONY AND IVORY/
Rainclouds
PAUL McCARTNEY
(A-side: with vocals by Stevie Wonder)

Columbia 18-02860
April 2, 1982 (March 29, 1982)

EBONY AND IVORY/
Rainclouds/Ebony and Ivory (solo version)
PAUL McCARTNEY
(A-side: with vocals by Stevie Wonder)

Columbia 44-02878 (12-inch single)
April 16, 1982

 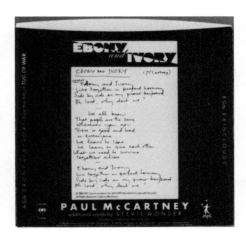

The long-awaited duet between pop music's two biggest paycheck recipients finally emerged in the spring of 1982 and immediately shot up the charts reportedly faster than any other single in more than a decade. While the critics were almost universal in their negative appraisal of this lyrical exercise in racial harmony, the general public and radio programmers around the country responded so favorably that the disc zoomed to the top of the charts for a multiple week stay.

Shortly after the 7-inch single was released, a special 12-inch version was issued which also contained the original solo vocal version of "Ebony and Ivory" by McCartney sans Wonder.

Billboard	CASH BOX	Record World
	①	

NOTE: After the record debuted at No. 40 for the week of 4/10/82 Record World ceased publication.

THE ALBUMS

1963–1982

INTRODUCING THE BEATLES
THE BEATLES

Vee Jay 1062
July 22, 1963

I Saw Her Standing There/Misery/
Anna/Chains/Boys/Love Me Do/P.S.
I Love You/Baby It's You/Do You Want
To Know a Secret/A Taste of Honey/
There's a Place/Twist and Shout

Despite the fact that two singles had already failed, Vee Jay went ahead and released the first album collection of Beatle songs in the U.S. As was the case with the singles, Vee Jay was once more faced with a reluctant and uninterested record-buying public in America, while the British album, PLEASE PLEASE ME, from which these tracks were taken, was setting sales records.

Too far ahead of their time? Or was Vee Jay merely stuck with a white elephant musical group? It would be another six months before the American people would be willing to embrace the lads from Liverpool.

MEET THE BEATLES
THE BEATLES

Capitol ST-2047
January 20, 1964

I Want to Hold Your Hand/I Saw Her
Standing There/This Boy/It Won't Be
Long/All I've Got to Do/All My
Loving/Don't Bother Me/Little Child/
Till There Was You/Hold Me Tight/I
Wanna Be Your Man/Not a Second
Time

After having passed on them a year before, Capitol Records finally took advantage of its EMI option and released their first gathering of Beatles songs, titled MEET THE BEATLES though most of the songs were actually from the group's second UK album, WITH THE BEATLES, and in spite of the fact that Vee Jay had already tried *introducing* the quartet.

Capitol launched the arrival of the Beatles to America in early 1964 with the largest single promotional campaign in the history of the record industry, and in doing so helped to fuel the initial monumental wave of a brand-new worldwide social disease, which now spread over the U.S.—*Beatlemania*.

Whether or not the promotion had anything to do with it, the Fab Four from Liverpool took America by storm, and this album led the way for most of early 1964. Every track of this LP gained saturation-level airplay, while all three charts zoomed it straight to the top.

Billboard

☆ 1

CASH BOX

(1)

Record World

| 1 |

INTRODUCING THE BEATLES
THE BEATLES

Vee Jay 1062
January 27, 1964

**I Saw Her Standing There/Misery/
Anna/Chains/Boys/Ask Me Why/
Please Please Me/Baby It's You/Do
You Want to Know a Secret/A Taste
of Honey/There's a Place/Twist and
Shout**

In an effort to make up for the failure of their 1963 outing, Vee Jay decided to rerelease their album and cash in on the newly forged Beatlemania sweeping the nation. Due to some publishing rights now controlled by Capitol, Vee Jay was forced to replace two songs on the album ("Love Me Do" and "P.S. I Love You") with two others ("Please Please Me" and "Ask Me Why"). Otherwise, this was the same album that had been put out six months earlier with no success at all.

This time, the album gained immediate airplay, and followed MEET THE BEATLES to the top of the charts, even managing to slip past it on *Record World* into the Number One slot.

2

CASH BOX
2

Record World
1

147

THE BEATLES WITH TONY SHERIDAN AND THEIR GUESTS
THE BEATLES featuring Tony Sheridan
(also: Tony Sheridan and the Beat Brothers; The Titans)

MGM SE-4215
February 3, 1964

My Bonnie/Cry for a Shadow/The Saints/Why/(additional tracks by Tony Sheridan and the Beat Brothers; The Titans)

This Beatles album contained all of one whole Beatles tune, an instrumental at that. The Beatles appear on just three additional cuts, backing up singer Tony Sheridan. The remainder of the album is by Tony Sheridan and the Beat Brothers (*not* the Beatles), and some group called the Titans. MGM didn't own very much of the Beatles catalog, but what little they did possess, they certainly attempted to make work. Integrity was seemingly tossed out of the window, as evidenced by the album cover, on which the Beatles' name takes up almost half of the total space.

The trick worked well enough to sucker several thousand buyers at the cash register, who obviously bought the album solely on the basis of the front cover, while neglecting to inspect the actual contents listed on the back. As an added sales incentive, this album was marketed with a green cover (the most common), a red cover, and a blue cover.

The charts noted their first major difference on the album charts—in this case, how much damage was caused to the public by this rip-off.

Billboard

68

CASH BOX

43

Record World

—

JOLLY WHAT! THE BEATLES AND FRANK IFIELD ON STAGE
THE BEATLES (and Frank Ifield)

Vee Jay 1085
February 26, 1964

Please Please Me/From Me to You/Ask Me Why/Thank You Girl/(additional tracks by Frank Ifield)

Vee Jay, wanting desperately to have more Beatles product on the market, slipped four tracks off INTRODUCING THE BEATLES and threw them onto this album of Frank Ifield recordings, making for certainly a most unusual, if not utterly ridiculous, "copulation."

Perhaps the inane cover artwork (drawing of an old man) kept more unsuspecting fans from being taken by this ruse. For the album's second pressing, Vee Jay adopted the artwork of their "Love Me Do" sleeve in hopes of stimulating slumping sales. However, by the time this second cover was ready to go, the album had already quit selling, so release of this second cover was extremely limited.

104

73

—

THE BEATLES' SECOND ALBUM
THE BEATLES

Capitol ST-2080
April 10, 1964

**Roll Over Beethoven/Thank You Girl/
You Really Got a Hold on Me/Devil in
Her Heart/Money/You Can't Do That/
Long Tall Sally/I Call Your Name/
Please Mr. Postman/I'll Get You/She
Loves You**

Even as MEET THE BEATLES topped the charts, Capitol issued their second collection of tunes, imaginatively titled THE BEATLES' SECOND ALBUM. Again, several songs were taken from the group's second English album, WITH THE BEATLES. Added to these in order to complete this offering were Swan's "She Loves You"/"I'll Get You" single and a couple of recently recorded numbers.

In any case, most Americans were hearing these songs for the very first time—and hearing them they were, as this album duplicated the total saturation level of radio airplay that MEET THE BEATLES had received, and quickly replaced it as the Number One album in the United States.

Billboard
☆ 1

CASH BOX
① 1

Record World
1

THE AMERICAN TOUR WITH ED RUDY
Ed Rudy interviews THE BEATLES

Radio Pulsebeat News Documentary No. 2
June 9, 1964

The American Tour with Ed Rudy/
Phone Interview

Newsman Ed Rudy became another of the many self-appointed "Fifth Beatles" during the group's first American visit in early 1964. He traveled with them on all of their stops in New York, Miami, and Washington, D.C. and recorded most of their press conferences. He then ventured into a recording studio and rerecorded himself asking all of the questions, which had, in fact, been asked by a wide variety of reporters. The answers given by the Beatles were spliced in. The result was an entire album of Ed Rudy "interviewing" the Beatles.

However questionable this effort obviously was, it turned out to be highly successful, as the album sold quite well, and for an interview album did outstandingly on the charts.

Billboard

CASH BOX
55

Record World
32

A HARD DAY'S NIGHT
THE BEATLES
(with soundtrack music by George Martin and orchestra)

United Artists UAS-6366
June 26, 1964

A Hard Day's Night/Tell Me Why/I'll Cry Instead/I'm Happy Just to Dance with You/I Should Have Known Better/ If I Fell/And I Love Her/Can't Buy Me Love/(additional tracks by George Martin and Orchestra)

United Artists not only had the rights to the Beatles' first motion picture, but also to the soundtrack album. Under the agreement with EMI/Capitol in the United States, they could however feature only the set of eight songs intended for use in the movie, and thus could not fill the remainder of the record with Beatles recordings. Thus, the album was padded out with instrumental versions of Beatles tunes by George Martin and his orchestra.

Even so, with only eight new Beatles tracks, the album became an instant super-success, saturating the airwaves and rising to the top spot on all three charts.

Billboard   **CASH BOX**   *Record World*

☆ 1   ① 1   ☐ 1

SOMETHING NEW
THE BEATLES

Capitol ST-2108
July 20, 1964

I'll Cry Instead/Things We Said Today/
Anytime at All/When I Get Home/Slow
Down/Matchbox/Tell Me Why/And I
Love Her/I'm Happy Just to Dance
With You/If I Fell/Komm, Gib Mir Diene
Hand

For Capitol's third album, songs from the motion picture *A Hard Day's Night* were coupled with various other new recordings, and rushed out a month after the United Artists soundtrack album hit the stores.

Apparently, the EMI–United Artists arrangement managed to allow Capitol the right to include no less than five of the official soundtrack album's eight Beatles songs on SOMETHING NEW. Four of the five tracks were immediately tossed on a pair of singles and rush released shortly after Capitol had already issued "A Hard Day's Night"/"I Should Have Known Better" as a single. The remaining movie track, "Can't Buy Me Love," had been served up as a Capitol single nearly four months previously. Although composed of one album and four singles, this gave Capitol, in one form or another, all eight of the soundtrack tunes to market concurrently with the U-A offering. Not a bad agreement for EMI.

Even with identical material, Capitol was able to enjoy yet another smash hit release by the Beatles, although SOMETHING NEW could never quite gain that something "extra" needed to knock A HARD DAY'S NIGHT out of the Number One position.

Billboard

☆ 2

CASH BOX

② 2

Record World

2

THE BEATLES VS. THE FOUR SEASONS
THE BEATLES (record one)
(The Four Seasons, record two)

Vee Jay DX-30
October 1, 1964

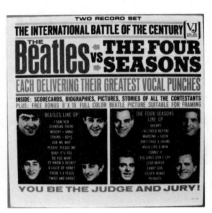

I Saw Her Standing There/Misery/ Anna/Chains/Boys/Ask Me Why/ Please Please Me/Baby It's You/Do You Want to Know A Secret/A Taste of Honey/There's a Place/Twist and Shout/(second record by the Four Seasons)

Vee Jay still sorely wished to release a true follow-up album to INTRODUCING THE BEATLES, but was unable to for the simple reason that they owned no further new material. Taking Beatles songs and combining them with tracks by other artists on the same record had not proved too successful, so Vee Jay decided simply to reissue the entire INTRODUCING THE BEATLES album with a new name and cover. Their initial effort in this area resulted in a most bizarre pairing with a Four Seasons album, in a special two-record set subtitled "The International Battle of the Century," complete with scorecard on back cover for track-by-track comparison and rating.

Needless to say, this album failed to catch many fans, who were already becoming very leery of non-Capitol Beatles albums, and disappeared before more were even aware of its existence.

Billboard

142

CASH BOX

Record World

AIN'T SHE SWEET
THE BEATLES
(also: THE BEATLES with Tony Sheridan, and the Swallows)

ATCO SD 33-169
October 5, 1964

Ain't She Sweet/Sweet Georgia Brown/Take Out Some Insurance On Me, Baby/Nobody's Child/(additional tracks by the Swallows)

Following the Top Twenty success of their "Ain't She Sweet" single, ATCO at last decided to cash in on the album market by issuing this album, which features the title track, plus three of the Beatles' other 1961 Hamburg numbers featuring singer Tony Sheridan, along with eight additional tracks (Beatles lovers) by a group called the Swallows.

Fortunately, American buyers were wising up, and this record did not sell.

SONGS, PICTURES AND STORIES OF THE FABULOUS BEATLES
THE BEATLES

Vee Jay 1092
October 12, 1964

I Saw Her Standing There/Misery/ Anna/Chains/Boys/Ask Me Why/ Please Please Me/Baby, It's You/Do You Want to Know a Secret/A Taste of Honey/There's a Place/Twist and Shout

Less than two weeks after the release of THE BEATLES VS. THE FOUR SEASONS, Vee Jay rushed out another repackage of INTRODUCING THE BEATLES, this time in a special fold-out cover with photos and biographies on the inside.

Notable was the fact that, as with THE BEATLES VS. THE FOUR SEASONS, Vee Jay didn't even bother to print new labels for the record. All copies of DX-30 and 1092 actually contained discs with 1062 labels, still stating INTRODUCING THE BEATLES as the title.

Regardless, the more alluring artwork of SONGS, PICTURES AND STORIES OF THE FABULOUS BEATLES managed to catch a few more Beatles fans off-guard, and the album sold well enough to make all three charts before people realized they were buying the same album for the fourth different time.

Billboard

63

CASH BOX
(100)

Record World
79

THE BEATLES' STORY
THE BEATLES

Capitol STBO-2222
November 23, 1964

(Narration and interviews) On Stage with The Beatles/How Beatlemania Began/Beatlemania in Action/Man Behind the Beatles—Brian Epstein/John Lennon/Who's a Millionaire/Beatles Will Be Beatles/Man Behind the Music—George Martin/George Harrison/A Hard Day's Night—Their First Movie/Paul McCartney/Sneaky Haircuts and More About Paul/Twist and Shout (excerpt from 1964 Hollywood Bowl tape)/The Beatles Look at Life/Victims of Beatlemania/Beatle Medley/Ringo Starr/Liverpool and All the World

Capitol decided to beat everyone else to the punch when it came to telling American Beatles fans and record buyers the true story of the group's rise from obscurity to fame. This double album featured interviews, commentary, snatches of Beatles songs (including a few seconds of "Twist and Shout" recorded live at their 1964 Hollywood Bowl concert), and a complete narration of their life stories.

The album sold quite well at first, until word got around that it not only failed to include any new songs, but in fact did not contain even one single complete song. Also, this two-record set carried a price higher than many fans were accustomed to, and eventually stalled out in the Top Ten on two of the charts, while just missing the Top Ten on the other.

7

CASH BOX

7

Record World

13

BEATLES '65
THE BEATLES

Capitol ST-2228
December 15, 1964

No Reply/I'm a Loser/Baby's in Black/
Rock and Roll Music/I'll Follow the
Sun/Mr. Moonlight/Honey Don't/I'll
Be Back/She's a Woman/I Feel Fine/
Everybody's Trying to Be My Baby

Taking songs from the English albums BEATLES FOR SALE and A HARD DAY'S NIGHT, plus adding the group's latest hit single, Capitol manufactured their fifth Beatles album, rushed out onto the market just in time for Christmas. What better gift than the Beatles newest album? Apparently everyone agreed, because this record zoomed to the top of the charts, selling faster than Christmas trees all over the country.

There was saturation-level airplay on the radio, and Beatlemania was obviously going to carry over into the new year of 1965.

CASH BOX

①

Record World

1

ED RUDY WITH NEW U.S. TOUR (THE BEATLES GREAT AMERICAN TOUR)
Ed Rudy interviews THE BEATLES

Radio Pulsebeat News L-1001/1002 (News Documentary No. 3) 1965

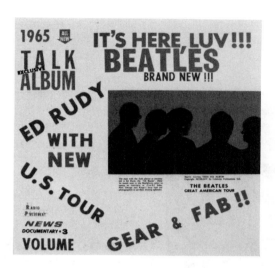

Ed Rudy with new U.S. Tour/Ed Rudy with new U.S. Tour

In 1965, Ed Rudy put together another legally questionable album of Beatles interviews, this time taken from press comments made during their second 1964 U.S. tour. It was produced in the same manner as the first had been, with Ed rerecording most of the questions himself.

The new record was not as widely circulated as the earlier effort had been, and it failed to receive the same kind of sales attention.

CASH BOX

Record World

THE EARLY BEATLES
THE BEATLES

Capitol ST-2309
March 22, 1965

Love Me Do/Twist and Shout/Anna/
Chains/Boys/Ask Me Why/Please
Please Me/P.S. I Love You/Baby It's
You/A Taste of Honey/Do You Want to
Know a Secret

Now that Capitol had finally acquired the Vee Jay tracks, they reissued this set of material for no less than the fifth time on an album in the United States.

With a couple of minor changes (Capitol eliminated "I Saw Her Standing There," "Misery," and "There's A Place," and reinstated "Love Me Do" and "P.S. I Love You" into the line-up), this album was once again tossed out to the hungry Beatles fans, who bought it all over again in enough numbers to move it into the Top Thirty on *Cash Box* and *Record World,* and the Top Fifty on *Billboard.*

Billboard

43

CASH BOX

(24)

Record World

29

BEATLES VI
THE BEATLES

Capitol ST-2358
June 14, 1965

Kansas City/Hey Hey Hey Hey//Eight Days a Week/You Like Me Too Much/Bad Boy/I Don't Want to Spoil the Party/Words of Love/What You're Doing/Yes It Is/Dizzy Miss Lizzie/Tell Me What You See/Every Little Thing

Capitol's seventh Beatles album was aptly titled BEATLES VI. Presumably, Capitol was not counting THE BEATLES' STORY as a full-fledged album, or could it be that they were not taking THE EARLY BEATLES into account? Whatever, Capitol this time went shopping and returned from England with material left over from BEATLES FOR SALE, along with tracks intended for the as-yet-unreleased HELP! album, in order to produce BEATLES VI. (In fact, Capitol was in such a hurry to release this album that the covers were printed before the final track running order had been decided—with the result that the first run of albums showed the track listing out of order and a disclaimer stating, "See label for correct playing order.")

Nevertheless, BEATLES VI rapidly filled the transistor radios of America, and shot to the top of the charts.

1

CASH BOX

1

Record World

1

HELP!
THE BEATLES
   (with soundtrack music by George Martin and orchestra)

Capitol SMAS-2386
August 13, 1965

Help!/The Night Before/You've Got to Hide Your Love Away/I Need You/Another Girl/Ticket to Ride/You're Gonna Lose That Girl/(additional tracks by George Martin and orchestra)

As the rest of the world received a brand new Beatles HELP! album with seven songs from the movie on one side, and seven additional new Beatles tunes on the other side, fans in the United States were treated to Capitol's own version of the motion picture soundtrack album, which included only the seven Beatles songs from the film and seven soundtrack instrumentals by George Martin and his orchestra as padding. Even John Lennon was reported to have been upset when he was informed of this "special movie souvenir package" (as it had been dubbed by Capitol).

   In the meantime, HELP! immediately became the top seller in the nation, and the seven lonely Beatles tunes had no need of any additional help in filling the ears of America's youth.

Billboard

☆ 1

CASH BOX

① 1

Record World

1

RUBBER SOUL
THE BEATLES

Capitol ST-2442
December 6, 1965

I've Just Seen a Face/Norwegian Wood (This Bird Has Flown)/You Won't See Me/Think for Yourself/The Word/ Michelle/It's Only Love/Girl/I'm Looking Through You/In My Life/Wait/ Run for Your Life

With this album, the Beatles really began to change the way pop records were made. RUBBER SOUL was hailed as the first *true album*, as opposed to merely a twelve-inch collection of random singles. The music on this disc showed a definite growth in the songwriting abilities of the Beatles, as the simple boy-girl themes were upgraded by complicated and intriguing lyrics, such as in "Norwegian Wood."

In addition to the now-common saturation level of radio airplay, RUBBER SOUL also earned the group a great deal of new respect from many long-time skeptics and critics, who up to this point had doubted the Beatles' ability to sustain, let alone improve upon, their Number One standing in the world.

Released just in time for Christmas (a Beatles trademark), this record soon topped all three charts with ease.

Billboard ☆ 1

CASH BOX ① 1

Record World 1

YESTERDAY . . . AND TODAY
THE BEATLES

Capitol ST-2553
June 15, 1966 (first cover edition)
June 20, 1966 (second cover edition)

**Drive My Car/I'm Only Sleeping/
Nowhere Man/Dr. Robert/Yesterday/
Act Naturally/And Your Bird Can Sing/
If I Needed Someone/We Can Work It
Out/What Goes On/Day Tripper**

This was the infamous "Butcher Cover" album, whose photo caused such a furor upon release that all copies were immediately recalled to the factory by Capitol and pasted over with a new, tamer pose. Capitol was also forced to recall and destroy thousands of dollars' worth of promotional posters and sales aids that also prominently displayed the allegedly offensive portrait.

Actually, the "Butcher" photo had served only as a personal commentary by the Beatles regarding Capitol's habit of tearing apart their carefully crafted British albums solely in order to churn out more "product" for the States. Thus, the "Butcher" pose was most appropriate for YESTERDAY . . . AND TODAY, which was made up entirely of leftover material from older albums, as well as new material from the as-yet-unreleased REVOLVER album.

In any case, YESTERDAY . . . AND TODAY soon commanded the Beatles' usual saturation level of airplay, while quickly climbing to the top spot on all of the charts.

Billboard

1

CASH BOX
①

Record World
1

REVOLVER
THE BEATLES

Capitol ST-2576
August 8, 1966

Taxman/Eleanor Rigby/Love You Too/
Here, There and Everywhere/Yellow
Submarine/She Said She Said/Good
Day Sunshine/For No One/I Want to
Tell You/Got to Get You Into My Life/
Tomorrow Never Knows

Released while YESTERDAY . . . AND TODAY topped the charts, REVOLVER was issued in the summer of 1966, and once more marked another giant step forward in the evolution of pop-rock music and the total-album concept. The next logical step beyond RUBBER SOUL, REVOLVER heightened the critical praise and acclaim as well as reaffirmed the public's enthusiasm and interest in the group.

With REVOLVER, George Harrison emerged more than on any previous album; and at the time, it was unthinkable that the Beatles could continue growing or expanding much further. In fact, REVOLVER was such an impressive work that even today many critics rate it one of the best, if not perhaps the single best, albums by the Beatles. (To fully appreciate this album, check out the complete version by picking up the UK release, which includes three additional songs, including two more Lennon numbers, which represent him better and make for a more well-rounded group offering than the pared down U.S. issue.)

Radio airplay was confident, constant, and congested as usual. The charts soon placed it atop everything else.

Billboard

CASH BOX

Record World

1

SGT. PEPPER'S LONELY HEARTS CLUB BAND
THE BEATLES

Capitol SMAS-2635
June 2, 1967

Sgt. Pepper's Lonely Hearts Club Band/With a Little Help from My Friends/Lucy in the Sky with Diamonds/Getting Better/Fixing a Hole/She's Leaving Home/Being for the Benefit of Mr. Kite/Within You Without You/When I'm Sixty-Four/Lovely Rita/Good Morning Good Morning/Sgt. Pepper's Lonely Hearts Club Band (reprise)/A Day in the Life

For those who thought REVOLVER could not be topped, SGT. PEPPER must have been the shock of their lives. Even for those who thought it could be topped, SGT. PEPPER still must have been a major shock. Never in the history of popular music has one single album had such an immediate and total impact on the entire music industry.

With SGT. PEPPER, the Beatles once again changed the entire course of pop-rock music, and reached new heights in songwriting maturity and musical experimentation. SGT. PEPPER heralded another set of social changes, as the appearance of the Beatles (mustaches, floral clothes, military uniforms, and so forth) also helped to spark another cultural youth revolution.

The summer of 1967 was the summer of love, and the airwaves were spearheaded once again by the sounds of the Beatles. The charts immediately reflected yet another multi-week top positioner.

Billboard
☆ 1

CASH BOX
① 1

Record World
1

MAGICAL MYSTERY TOUR
THE BEATLES

Capitol SMAL-2835
November 27, 1967

Magical Mystery Tour/The Fool on the Hill/Flying/Blue Jay Way/Your Mother Should Know/I Am the Walrus/Hello Goodbye/Strawberry Fields Forever/Penny Lane/Baby, You're a Rich Man/All You Need Is Love

Released in the UK as a double EP, the songs from the TV special of the same name were joined by Capitol with the three singles released by the group in 1967. The result was a full album of material for American buyers.

Critics seemed divided between those who felt that this album was not up to SGT. PEPPER, and those who realized that this album was not really a true album at all, but pointed out anyway that the songs from the TV special were quite possibly just as good as, if not better in some cases than, the tracks on SGT. PEPPER.

Debates aside, this record soon became the mainstay of U.S. radio stations for the holidays, and had no trouble in giving the Beatles the top spot on the charts for another Christmas season.

Billboard

★ 1

CASH BOX

① 1

Record World

1

UNFINISHED MUSIC NO. 1—TWO VIRGINS
JOHN LENNON AND YOKO ONO

Apple/Tetragrammaton T-5001
November 11, 1968

Two Virgins No.1/Together/Two Virgins No. 2/Two Virgins No. 3/Two Virgins No.4/Two Virgins No. 5/Two Virgins No. 6/Hushabye Hushabye/ Two Virgins No. 7/Two Virgins No. 8/ Two Virgins No. 9/Two Virgins No. 10

This album holds the distinction of being perhaps the most-talked-about-yet-least-listened-to album in pop history. For the record, this album was actually the soundtrack companion to the seldom-seen John and Yoko film of the same name. If the film is anything like the sounds on the records, it is obvious why it is so seldom seen.

However, it was the cover—*that* cover—that gained all of the attention. It's not every day that one gets to see a nude Beatle and his girlfriend, from both A and B sides! The press had a field day, even becoming so mixed up that for a time it was reported that the upcoming Beatles album was supposed to feature this cover (and the plain white cover of THE BEATLES was cited incorrectly as support for that misconception).

Capitol wouldn't touch it, so Apple gave it to Tetragrammaton in the States, and it was finally issued in a plain brown wrapper. It sold, mainly as a curiosity, though the charts strongly disagreed in their accounts of those sales. Airplay was nil.

Billboard

124

CASH BOX

82

Record World

56

THE BEATLES ("White Album")
THE BEATLES

Apple SWBO-101
November 25, 1968

Back in the U.S.S.R./Dear Prudence/ Glass Onion/Ob-La-Di Ob-La-Da/ Wild Honey Pie/The Continuing Story of Bungalow Bill / While My Guitar Gently Weeps/Happiness Is a Warm Gun/Martha My Dear/I'm So Tired/ Blackbird/Piggies/Rocky Racoon/ Don't Pass Me By/Why Don't We Do It in the Road/I Will/Julia/Birthday/ Yer Blues/Mother Nature's Son/Everybody's Got Something to Hide Except Me and My Monkey/Sexy Sadie/Helter Skelter/Long, Long, Long/Revolution I/Honey Pie/Savoy Truffle/Cry Baby Cry/Revolution 9/Good Night

Issued in a blank white cover, in stark contrast to the lavish SGT. PEPPER and MAGICAL MYSTERY TOUR artwork, this album allowed the Beatles once again to stun the rock world. After all, nobody releases an album with thirty songs on it. But the Beatles were definitely somebody and by doing just that, they proved beyond any doubt that they still had some new punches to throw, and intended to stay on top of the music world.

The Beatles returned to rock 'n' roll with this album, and they managed to cover and parody almost every musical style in existence, as well as turn out some classic new sounds of their own. The entire effort was overwhelming, and for some of the critics and public it was all too massive to comprehend and appreciate fully.

This also marked the Beatles' first album on their own Apple label, distributed in the United States by Capitol, and, not surprisingly, was released just in time for Christmas, enabling it to skyrocket to the top of the charts and shove all Christmas carols off the airwaves.

Billboard

☆ 1

CASH BOX

(1)

Record World

| 1 |

WONDERWALL MUSIC
GEORGE HARRISON

Apple ST-3350
December 2, 1968

Microbes/Red Lady Too//Tabla and Pakavaj/In the Park//Drilling a Home/ Guru Vandana//Greasy Legs/Ski-ing and Gat Kirwani/Dream Scene//Party Seacombe//Love Scene/Crying// Cowboy Museum//Fantasy Sequins/ Glass Box//On the Bed/Wonderwall to Be Here/Singing Om

George Harrison's first solo album was not really a true George Harrison album; he would save that for ALL THINGS MUST PASS two years later. WONDERWALL MUSIC was simply an album of soundtrack music that George wrote and recorded in late 1967 and early 1968 for the motion picture *Wonderwall*.

Because of the way George's name appeared on the cover, and because neither the front nor back cover provided any listing of song titles or liner notes to inform otherwise, many people rushed out to buy what they assumed to be a solo album of pop-rock music by one of the Beatles. Instead, they purchased the soundtrack album of a movie that most people had never even heard of, let alone seen.

The album, for the reasons noted, sold well enough to crack the Top Fifty on all three major charts.

Billboard

49

CASH BOX

39

Record World

33

YELLOW SUBMARINE
THE BEATLES (with George Martin soundtrack music)

Apple SW-153
January 13, 1969

Yellow Submarine/Only a Northern Song/All Together Now/Hey Bulldog/ It's All Too Much/All You Need Is Love/(additional tracks by George Martin and orchestra)

To coincide with the release of their long-awaited animated motion picture, *Yellow Submarine*, the Beatles released a soundtrack album, one side filled with Beatles songs from the movie, and one side filled with soundtrack music by George Martin and his orchestra.

Originally, the album was to have contained many of the older Beatles songs included in the movie (e.g. "Nowhere Man"), which would no doubt have made for a more satisfying Beatles product. However, the decision was made to delete several of the older numbers and fill side two of the record with incidental George Martin music.

Both the album and the motion picture became huge successes, with YELLOW SUBMARINE being kept out of the top spot on two of the charts only by the Beatles' own album, THE BEATLES.

CASH BOX

③

Record World

2

UNFINISHED MUSIC NO. 2—LIFE WITH THE LIONS
JOHN LENNON AND YOKO ONO

Zapple ST-3357
May 26, 1969

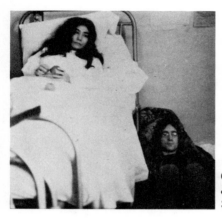

Cambridge 1969/No Bed for Beatle John/Baby's Heartbeat/Two Minutes Silence/Radio Play

In the spring of 1969, John and Yoko followed up their TWO VIRGINS album by releasing LIFE WITH THE LIONS, another collection of noises, sounds, silences, and screams that seemed to be testing the limits of what Beatles fans would be willing to spend their money on. Basically, it was simply continued experimentation, with new forms of musical and non-musical expression being tried out by John and Yoko, who wanted to share this new frontier with their fans. This album was the first on the Zapple label, a new subdivision of the Apple label, designed specifically to handle such "special" product.

Airplay was non-existent, but the record sold well enough to make all three charts, although *Billboard* seemed to have considerably more doubt about it than the other two.

Billboard

☆ 174

CASH BOX

(118)

Record World

□ 124

ELECTRONIC SOUND
GEORGE HARRISON

Zapple ST-3358
May 26, 1969

Under the Mersey Wall/No Time or Space

Once again, George wrote and produced and played on a record that could hardly be called a solo Harrison album. This time out, George seemed to catch a case of the "Lennons" and put together this equally bizarre collection of electronic sounds and noises. George however couldn't help but show his sense of humor over the project, going so far as to include liner notes on the inner sleeve stating, "There are a lot of people around making a lot of noise . . . here's some more."

This was the second and last album on the short-lived Zapple label. Despite the claim that Zapple Records would feature a special reduced price tag, it hit the racks (along with LIFE WITH THE LIONS) at full $5.98 list.

ELECTRONIC SOUND quickly sank into obscurity, with only *Billboard* allowing it barely to slip into the Top 200.

191

ABBEY ROAD
THE BEATLES

Apple SO-383
October 1, 1969

Come Together/Something/Maxwell's Silver Hammer/Oh! Darling/Octopus's Garden/I Want You (She's So Heavy)/Here Comes the Sun/Because/You Never Give Me Your Money/Sun King/Mean Mr. Mustard/Polythene Pam/She Came in Through the Bathroom Window/Golden Slumbers/Carry That Weight/The End/Her Majesty

Disheartened with the GET BACK project started at the beginning of the year, the Beatles regrouped one last time for a series of mid-1969 sessions, during which they again proved their amazing ability to achieve the impossible against all odds, and recorded not only their last album together, but also another classic work in true SGT. PEPPER/REVOLVER fashion.

ABBEY ROAD met with the most hearty and universal praise of any Beatles album since SGT. PEPPER, and many critics went on to proclaim it their *best ever*. Certainly, the medley of songs on side two will stand the test of time.

Radio airplay and cash register sales continued to prove beyond any doubt the group's worldwide Number One status. Though the GET BACK recordings would later emerge as LET IT BE, this was in fact the Beatles' final work together, and stands as a true and lasting final crowning achievement.

Billboard
☆ 1

CASH BOX
(1)

Record World
[1]

WEDDING ALBUM
JOHN ONO LENNON AND YOKO ONO LENNON

Apple SMAX-3361
October 20, 1969

John and Yoko/Amsterdam

Seven months after the fact, John and Yoko celebrated their marriage by releasing this special WEDDING ALBUM, a super-deluxe boxed-set package, complete with birth certificate, plastic photo of a wedding cake, and a book of newspaper and press clippings from all over the world denoting their various escapades. The entire package was beautifully put together, and was quite an impressive souvenir. The album itself featured one side on which John and Yoko each repeat the other's name for twenty-three minutes, while the other side offered bits and pieces of interviews and conversations from their bed-in in Amsterdam.

The mere gigantic physical size of the boxed set caused many stores to pass on it at the time, and the public's uncertainty about the whole effort was reflected in the charts.

Billboard ★ 178

CASH BOX ⊖

Record World 108

LIVE PEACE IN TORONTO 1969
PLASTIC ONO BAND

Apple SW-3362
December 12, 1969 (December 15, 1969)

Blue Suede Shoes/Money/Dizzy Miss Lizzie/Yer Blues/Cold Turkey/Give Peace a Chance/Don't Worry Kyoko (Mummy's Only Looking for Her Hand in the Snow)/John, John (Let's Hope For Peace)

At last, a John Lennon solo album to feature rock 'n' roll—in this case, a historic recording of the live concert appearance by the Plastic Ono Band at the Toronto Peace Festival and Rock 'N' Roll Revival on September 13, 1969. It was John's first live concert performance in over three years, and he never sounded better.

Reportedly, this album was prompted into release only after a bootleg version began circulating at the time. Whatever the reason, it was great to hear one of the Beatles singing live (the first live Beatle-singing on record). Initial copies of the album included a free calendar.

Billboard gave John his first solo Top Ten hit, while the other two charts awarded him Top Twenty status.

Billboard

☆ 10

CASH BOX

(18)

Record World

[18]

HEY JUDE (THE BEATLES AGAIN)
THE BEATLES

Apple SW-385 (SO-385)
February 26, 1970 (February 23, 1970)

Can't Buy Me Love/I Should Have Known Better/Paperback Writer/Rain/ Lady Madonna/Revolution/Hey Jude/ Old Brown Shoe/Don't Let Me Down/ The Ballad of John and Yoko

In January 1970, Apple sent out, then almost immediately recalled, promo copies of the GET BACK album. Following this, the decision was quickly made to issue this new album, enabling Capitol to fill the orders already taken for GET BACK. Hence, this collection of never-before-found-on-any-album tracks was assembled and rushed onto the market.

At first, the album was titled THE BEATLES AGAIN, and featured the reverse of the design of the eventual HEY JUDE cover (that is, the front cover photo of AGAIN became the back cover photo of HEY JUDE, and the back cover photo became the front cover photo). Initial copies of the HEY JUDE album featured labels still stating THE BEATLES AGAIN, with original catalog designation SO-385.

Airplay was fairly heavy for this album, especially considering that the tracks were anywhere from one to six years old, that ABBEY ROAD was still high on the charts, and that this was the first U.S. compilation of old material. Even so, this fill-in Beatles album went on to become one of their all-time biggest sellers, managing to hit Number One on *Record World* and No. 2 on the other charts.

Billboard

CASH BOX

(2)

Record World

| 1 |

McCARTNEY
PAUL McCARTNEY

Apple SMAS-3363
April 20, 1970 (April 17, 1970)

The Lovely Linda/That Would Be Something/Valentine Day/Every Night/Hot as Sun/Glasses/Junk/Man We Was Lonely/Oo You/Momma Miss America/Teddy Boy/Singalong Junk/ Maybe I'm Amazed/Kreen-Akrore

McCARTNEY, appropriately enough, was the much-heralded debut solo offering from ex-Beatle Paul McCartney. This homemade (literally!) effort was decidedly simple, but nonetheless a harmless vehicle for Paul, who used it as his own declaration of independence from the Beatles. Perhaps everyone just expected a bit more from Paul, especially following the production job turned in on ABBEY ROAD.

Just the same, it was enormously successful in spite of sales competition from the Beatles LET IT BE, which soon followed. Airplay was very heavy, and the charts were in total agreement in ranking it Number One.

Billboard

☆ 1

CASH BOX

① 1

Record World

1

SENTIMENTAL JOURNEY
RINGO STARR

Apple SW-3365
April 24, 1970 (April 20, 1970)

Sentimental Journey/Night and Day/
Whispering Grass (Don't Tell the
Trees)/Bye Bye Blackbird/I'm a Fool to
Care/Stardust/Blue, Turning Grey
Over You/Love Is a Many Splen-
doured Thing/Dream/You Always Hurt
the One You Love/Have I Told You Lately
That I Love You/Let the Rest of the
World Go By

For his solo debut, Ringo decided to test his overall singing abilities by doing cover versions of a dozen or so standard tunes, most of which dated back to the forties. In an attempt to offer even more variety, he employed a different producer for each track. Still, the entire project seemed a most unusual choice for Ringo, though he said later that he did it mainly to please his mother; and it's hard to fault a guy for trying to please his mom.

Radio airplay was virtually nil, though the album sold quite well considering all.

Billboard

⭐ 22

CASH BOX

㉑

Record World

20

IN THE BEGINNING
THE BEATLES
(also: THE BEATLES featuring Tony Sheridan; Tony Sheridan and the Beat Brothers)

Polydor 24-4504
Capitol SKAO-93199 (Capitol Record Club issue)
May 4, 1970

Ain't She Sweet/Cry for a Shadow/ My Bonnie/Take Out Some Insurance on Me, Baby/Sweet Georgia Brown/ The Saints/Why/Nobody's Child/ (additional tracks by Tony Sheridan and the Beat Brothers)

It seemed as though the only time this batch of Beatles/Tony Sheridan tracks ever surfaced was when there happened to be a new Beatles album with which to coincide its release. So wouldn't you know it, Polydor decided to rerelease these recordings just in time to hit the market with Apple's new LET IT BE album. But at least Polydor included all eight of the Hamburg-recorded songs with the Beatles backing up singer Tony Sheridan, though they missed the date by a year, giving their vintage as circa 1960, when it should have been 1961. As usual, these numbers were padded out by additional filler from Tony and the Beat Brothers.

The album was packaged nicely enough and even included some early photos of the Beatles. It sold well enough to climb up the charts a bit, even cracking the Top 100 on *Cash Box*.

Billboard

117

CASH BOX

94

Record World

139

LET IT BE
THE BEATLES

Apple AR-34001
May 18, 1970

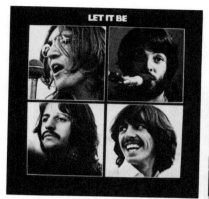

Two of Us/I Dig a Pony/Across the Universe/I Me Mine/Dig It/Let It Be/ Maggie Mae/I've Got a Feeling/One After 909/The Long and Winding Road/For You Blue/Get Back

LET IT BE, the soundtrack album for the motion picture, featured material which had largely been recorded in January 1969, and which, under the original project title GET BACK, had been mixed and scheduled for release several times between the summer of 1969 and early 1970 (radio stations had actually been sent copies of the album on these various occasions—leading to the availability of bootleg versions of the record long before the final commercial edition was released). After numerous unsuccessful mixes, Phil Spector was given the tapes and allowed to reconstruct the entire record.

In the end, GET BACK became LET IT BE, and despite the confusion and disillusionment over the breakup of the Beatles (Paul had officially announced the split just a few weeks prior to this album's release), both the album and the movie became big hits (though the public and the critics seemed divided in their opinions as to whether Spector had salvaged or destroyed the album). Radio airplay was again at saturation level, and the charts were unanimous in their Number One acknowledgment.

1

CASH BOX
1

Record World
1

BEAUCOUPS OF BLUES
RINGO STARR

Apple SMAS-3368
September 28, 1970

Beaucoups of Blues/Love Don't Last Long/Fastest Growing Heartache in the West/Without Her/Woman of the Night/I'd Be Talking All the Time/$15 Draw/Wine, Women and Loud Happy Songs/I Wouldn't Have You Any Other Way/Loser's Lounge / Waiting / Silent Homecoming

For his second solo album, Ringo once again tackled a project that he personally had always wanted to do. This time he went to Nashville and recorded an album of country and western numbers with producer Pete Drake and some of Nashville's top session players. However, Ringo was faced with the dilemma that on the one hand his record-buying public consisted of pop-rock music buyers who were not that enthusiastic about a total country and western album, and on the other hand country and western music fans and radio stations wanted little to do with an ex-Beatle.

Not surprisingly, the album gained hardly any airplay, and fared less well in the charts than had his first album.

Billboard

☆ 65

CASH BOX

(31)

Record World

[38]

ALL THINGS MUST PASS
(with free bonus LP: APPLE JAM)
GEORGE HARRISON

Apple STCH-639
November 27, 1970 (November 30, 1970)

I'd Have You Anytime/My Sweet Lord/
Wah-Wah/Isn't It a Pity (version one)/
What Is Life/If Not for You/Behind That
Locked Door/Let It Down/Run of the
Mill/Beware of Darkness/Apple
Scruffs/Ballad of Sir Frankie Crisp (Let
It Roll)/Awaiting on You All/All Things
Must Pass/I Dig Love/Art of Dying/Isn't It a Pity (version two)/Hear Me
Lord   (APPLE JAM) Out of the Blue/It's Johnny's Birthday/Plug Me In/I
Remember Jeep/Thanks for the Pepperoni

When George Harrison finally emerged from the shadow of the Beatles, and more specifically, the shadow of John Lennon and Paul McCartney, he did so with an almost unbelievably ambitious and impressive collection of his own songs.

ALL THINGS MUST PASS was the result of several years' worth of tunes, many of which had been planned for various Beatles albums, but were invariably passed over in favor of Lennon and McCartney works. (The title song, "All Things Must Pass," though assumed by most to have been a custom-penned statement on the breakup of the group, was in fact first recorded by the Beatles during their January 1969 GET BACK sessions.) With this release, George more than proved to any remaining doubters that his talent was equal to that of Lennon and McCartney. This double set of Harrisongs also included a third bonus album of jam session outtakes, which featured some very inspired guitar playing by George, backed by his all-star cast of session players.

ALL THINGS MUST PASS immediately dominated the radiowaves during the 1970 Christmas season, and soon topped all three charts with ease.

★
1

CASH BOX
(1)

Record World

1

JOHN LENNON/PLASTIC ONO BAND
JOHN LENNON/PLASTIC ONO BAND

Apple SW-3372
December 11, 1970 (December 9, 1970)

Mother/Hold On/I Found Out/Working Class Hero/Isolation/Remember/Love/Well Well Well/Look at Me/God/My Mummy's Dead

The first *real* solo album from John Lennon, ex-Beatle. This highly personal statement still stands as perhaps the strongest single effort by any of the former Beatles on their own. Stark, frank, and totally open in content, the pain was almost too much for most to bear. As one reviewer noted, the initial listening to this album could be compared to having just been hit by an atomic bomb—it was that devastating.

The album gained fairly favorable reviews and sold quite well, but airplay was not that heavy, due in part to the lack of a strong-selling single (John had opted for "Mother" rather than the more potentially commercial "Love"). This probably figured in the album's failing to hit the top of the charts, although *Record World* did elevate John right behind George, with the two former Beatles occupying back-to-back positions at the top of the chart.

Billboard

6

CASH BOX

4

Record World

2

RAM
PAUL AND LINDA McCARTNEY

Apple SMAS-3375
May 17, 1971

Too Many People/3 Legs/Ram On/
Dear Boy//Uncle Albert/Admiral
Halsey//Smile Away/Heart of the
Country/Monkberry Moon Delight/Eat
at Home/Long Haired Lady/Ram On/
The Back Seat of My Car

For Paul's second solo album, he gave full status to wife Linda, causing a monumental heap of vicious and unfair criticism to be thrown his way. On RAM, a totally New York studio effort with top session players, Paul actually turned in some fine numbers, ranging from some hard-driving rockers to the normal variety of McCartney ballads and occasional throw-aways. But for much of the public and many of the critics, RAM was earmarked as "bubble-gum" music.

It was nevertheless highly popular and successful in sales and airplay, and brought forth one unanimous hit single, the chart-topping "Uncle Albert/Admiral Halsey." Likewise, the charts were united in their solid No. 2 raking for RAM, behind Carole King's TAPESTRY, the biggest-selling album ever up to that time.

Billboard

☆ 2

CASH BOX

(2)

Record World

[2]

IMAGINE
JOHN LENNON/PLASTIC ONO BAND

Apple SW-3379
September, 9, 1971 (September 7, 1971)

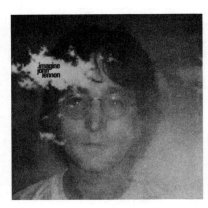

Imagine/Crippled Inside/Jealous Guy/
It's So Hard/I Don't Want to Be a
Soldier/Give Me Some Truth/Oh My
Love/How Do You Sleep/How/Oh
Yoko

John followed his highly personal and pain-afflicted JOHN LENNON/PLASTIC ONO BAND album with a more commercial offering. IMAGINE would prove to be John's most successful solo album, paced by the classic title song, wisely selected as the single. Even the critics agreed that the album, while not reaching the intense emotional level of the previous record, offered the listener some of the most beautiful and well-balanced songs John ever wrote.

The winning combination of strong sales and heavy airplay resulted in the unanimous Number One ranking on all three charts this time around.

Billboard

CASH BOX

Record World

1

WILD LIFE
WINGS

Apple SW-3386
December 8, 1971

Mumbo/Bip Bop/Love Is Strange/Wild
Life/Some People/Never Know/I Am
Your Singer/Tomorrow/Dear Friend

Following the attacks on RAM, Paul surfaced in late 1971 with a new band, Wings, and a new album, WILD LIFE, which had been recorded in just one week. To most, it sounded like it. The album was simply a bit too rushed, but with some care might have overcome many of its deficiencies. With only eight tracks, it also suffered from having not very much going for it out of the gate, and it must be noted that no single was pulled from the disc, an indication that there simply wasn't one track strong enough to carry the load, though it was said that the reggae remake of "Love Is Strange" was almost issued as a seven-incher.

Airplay was only mild at best, while the charts noted the record's Top Ten earnings.

10

CASH BOX
6

Record World
9

CONCERT FOR BANGLA DESH
GEORGE HARRISON and friends (with RINGO STARR)

Apple STCX-3385
December 20, 1971

Wah-Wah/My Sweet Lord/Awaiting on You All/Beware of Darkness/While My Guitar Gently Weeps/Here Comes the Sun/Something/Bangla Desh (Harrison)/It Don't Come Easy (Starr)/(additional tracks featuring Bob Dylan, Leon Russell, Billy Preston)

On August 1, 1971, George Harrison assembled some of the biggest names in rock music for a benefit concert in New York's Madison Square Garden, which resulted in the release of a film and album of the event. George was joined by fellow ex-Beatle Ringo Starr, along with Bob Dylan, Eric Clapton, Leon Russell, Billy Preston, Badfinger, and a cast of thousands in one of the greatest concert extravaganzas in the history of rock 'n' roll.

Contract difficulties delayed the album's release until Christmas, which actually may have worked in its favor. Radio airplay was fairly heavy on selected cuts, and despite its three-album "no discount" price tag, still sold well enough to top the chart at *Record World,* and almost do the same on the other two.

Billboard
☆ 2

CASH BOX
② 2

Record World
1

SOMETIME IN NEW YORK CITY
(with free bonus LP: LIVE JAM)
JOHN AND YOKO/PLASTIC ONO BAND

Apple SVBB-3392
June 12, 1972 (June 19, 1972)

Woman Is the Nigger of the World/ Sisters O Sisters/Attica State/Born in a Prison/New York City/Sunday Bloody Sunday/The Luck of the Irish/ John Sinclair/Angela/We're All Water (LIVE JAM) Cold Turkey/Don't Worry Kyoko/Well (Baby Please Don't Go)/Jamrag/Scumbag/Au

From the dreamy visions of IMAGINE, John (and Yoko) focused their sights on the harsh realities of social and political strife in America and around the world, and turned out a collection of slogans, themes, and anthems. SOMETIME IN NEW YORK CITY was the result, and the album immediately drew severely negative reviews. In addition to complaining about the rather clichéd lyrical treatments, many critics went so far as to question the musical merits of most of the tunes as well. Unfortunately overlooked was the track "New York City," a more or less updated sequel to "The Ballad of John and Yoko," which might have made for a very successful single, as opposed to the more or less nationally banned "Woman Is the Nigger of the World." Of course, John was never one to place his commercial talents above his personal statements or beliefs.

Included was the "free" bonus LIVE JAM album (cleverly used to camouflage the hike in the list price to $6.98), which had almost been released on its own in December 1971/January 1972, and would have featured early acoustic versions of "Attica State" and "Luck of the Irish" in addition to the assorted historical live material.

Airplay was almost non-existent, and the charts disagreed only about how badly John fared on this outing.

Billboard   **CASH BOX**   **Record World**

48   26   30

THE BEATLES 1962–1966
THE BEATLES

Apple SKBO-3403
April 2, 1973

Love Me Do/Please Please Me/From Me to You/She Loves You/I Want to Hold Your Hand/All My Loving/Can't Buy Me Love/A Hard Day's Night/And I Love Her/Eight Days a Week/I Feel Fine/Ticket to Ride/Yesterday/Help!/You've Got to Hide Your Love Away/We Can Work It Out/Day Tripper/Drive My Car/Norwegian Wood (This Bird Has Flown)/Nowhere Man/Michelle/In My Life/Girl/Paperback Writer/Eleanor Rigby/Yellow Submarine

Long overdue, to say the least, this "greatest hits" collection was finally gathered and issued only after an unauthorized set of the same had been packaged and sold via TV advertisements around the country.

This first of the two-volume set of double albums released simultaneously covered the Beatles' early period. As such, it was primarily made up of their hit singles, which revived the airplay of many of these "oldies" for the first time since the break-up of the group and helped to fuel the start of a renewed wave of Beatlemania in 1973. *Cash Box* gave the Number One ranking to this volume, while on the other two charts it trailed slightly the 1967–1970 set.

Billboard

CASH BOX

Record World

4

THE BEATLES 1967–1970
THE BEATLES

Apple SKBO-3404
April 2, 1973

Strawberry Fields Forever/Penny Lane/Sgt. Pepper's Lonely Hearts Club Band/With a Little Help from My Friends/Lucy in the Sky with Diamonds/A Day in the Life/All You Need Is Love/I Am the Walrus/Hello Goodbye/The Fool on the Hill/Magical Mystery Tour/Lady Madonna/Hey Jude/Revolution/Back in the U.S.S.R./While My Guitar Gently Weeps/Ob-La-Di Ob-La-Da/Get Back/Don't Let Me Down/The Ballad of John and Yoko/Old Brown Shoe/Here Comes the Sun/Come Together/Something/Octopus's Garden/Let It Be/Across the Universe/The Long and Winding Road

The second half of this two-volume set of "greatest hits" covered the group's later period, from experimentation to split, and included not only the period's continued string of hit singles but many album tracks as well.

Only the Beatles would need a *pair* of double albums to handle their wealth of material. In addition to being packaged in similar covers, they were just as often bought in tandem as purchased separately. After all, who only wanted *half* of the Beatles' career?

As with the earlier set, radio interest in their later material once again greatly increased. While on the charts, if there was a slight difference in the audience's preference, then the nod went to this collection, reaching Number One on *Billboard* and *Record World*, while coming in behind the 1962–1966 set on *Cash Box*.

Billboard	CASH BOX	Record World
☆ 1	②	1

RED ROSE SPEEDWAY
PAUL McCARTNEY AND WINGS

Apple SMAL-3409
April 30, 1973 (April 22, 1973)

Big Barn Bed/My Love/Get on the Right Thing/One More Kiss/Little Lamb Dragonfly/Single Pigeon/When the Night/Loup (1st Indian on the Moon)//medley: Hold Me Tight/Lazy Dynamite/Hands of Love/Power Cut

Coming a year and a half after WILD LIFE, RED ROSE SPEEDWAY at least gave hope for better things to come from Wings. A marked improvement all around, this album was nevertheless a very uncertain offering. Originally meant to be a double album, with live tracks included, it was pared down to a single release by EMI, who were at this point growing a bit unsure of Paul's sagging reputation and sales potential.

With a sigh of relief all around, this album was highly successful, and even managed to gather in a fair share of favorable reviews. The monster hit pop ballad single "My Love" helped to pace it to the top of all three hit parades, as well as to receive a fairly heavy amount of airplay.

CASH BOX

Record World

1

1

1

LIVING IN THE MATERIAL WORLD
GEORGE HARRISON

Apple SMAS-3410
May 29, 1973

Give Me Love (Give Me Peace on Earth)/Sue Me, Sue You Blues/The Light That Has Lighted the World/ Don't Let Me Wait Too Long/Who Can See It/Living in the Material World/ The Lord Loves the One (That Loves the Lord)/Be Here Now/Try Some, Buy Some/The Day the World Gets 'Round/That Is All

George's first studio album in more than two and a half years was certainly a long-awaited and much-anticipated event. *Rolling Stone* had first reported that the album was originally set for December 20, 1972, release, under the title THE MAGIC IS HERE AGAIN (co-produced by Harrison and Eric Clapton), and sporting a cover photo of George in black and white, playing a rainbow-colored guitar. Shortly thereafter, various rock journals announced a January or February expected release, with the title THE LIGHT THAT HAS LIGHTED THE WORLD (and the leadoff single to be the song of the same name, possibly Apple 1860).

Finally, almost six months later, LIVING IN THE MATERIAL WORLD emerged. The music was top notch, though some critics were not too kind. Overall, George still enjoyed his status as the *most-favored* ex-Beatle in terms of popularity and press, and this led to the almost immediate chart-topping success of the album, which replaced Paul's RED ROSE SPEEDWAY in the Number One slot, thus making for the third back-to-back Beatle-related album to maintain that position.

Airplay was very heavy, paced by the Number One single, "Give Me Love." A second single, "Don't Let Me Wait Too Long" (Apple 1866), was almost issued, but never did materialize.

1

CASH BOX

1

Record World

1

LIVE AND LET DIE

Original Soundtrack featuring title track by **PAUL McCARTNEY AND WINGS** and score by George Martin and his orchestra

United Artists LA-100G
July 2, 1973

Live and Let Die/(additional tracks by George Martin and orchestra)

This wasn't really a McCartney and Wings album, but the group did perform the title track, and their name was prominently displayed on the cover in such a way that for many record buyers it was thought to be a Wings album.

As the title tune for the James Bond movie, McCartney's "Live and Let Die" certainly did the job. Both the song and the movie were super hits, and helped to feed McCartney's rising popularity at the time. The rest of the album featured a fine George Martin score, and it was nice to see Paul cross paths with his old producer again.

The album didn't get any airplay except for the Wings single, but between that and the movie's huge box office, enough people bought the album to make it a Top Twenty entry.

Billboard

☆ 17

CASH BOX

20

Record World

17

RINGO
RINGO STARR

Apple SWAL-3413
October 31, 1973 (October 15, 1973)

I'm The Greatest/Hold On/Photograph/Sunshine Life for Me (Sail Away Raymond)/You're Sixteen/Oh My My/Step Lightly/Six O'Clock/Devil Woman/You and Me (Babe) *Later pressings changed title to "Have You Seen My Baby"*

This was not only Ringo's first rock 'n' roll album, but also the very first record since the break-up to feature all four former Beatles. Produced by Richard Perry, RINGO captured that all-too-fleeting spirit, and served up a most satisfying round of varied pop and rock tunes, along with some fine ballads, and of course, the by now customary country and western number.

The album was very well received by both critics and public, and perhaps knowing that two and sometimes three Beatles were playing together on some of these songs helped to make it all seem extra special. Whatever the reasons, it was Ringo's time to shine at long last, and the richness of material led to the first solo Beatle album from which no fewer than three singles ("Photograph," "You're Sixteen," and "Oh My My") were pulled. Airplay ranged from extremely heavy to saturation levels in most markets, and it zoomed up the charts, hitting the top spot on both *Cash Box* and *Record World*, and just missing on *Billboard*.

CASH BOX

① 1

Record World

| 1 |

MIND GAMES
JOHN LENNON

Apple SW-3414
October 31, 1973 (October 30, 1973)

Mind Games/Tight A$/Aisumasen
(I'm Sorry)/One Day at a Time/Bring
on the Lucie (Freeda Peeple)/Nutopian
International Anthem/Intuition/Out the
Blue/Only People/I Know (I Know)/You
Are Here/Meat City

Following SOMETIME IN NEW YORK CITY, John returned a year later with MIND GAMES, crafted in almost carbon copy format to that of IMAGINE, a similarity that many critics noted at the time, although all agreed that it was a major step back—in the right direction. Actually, MIND GAMES boasted many songs worthy of more merit than they had garnered on first review.

John certainly would have liked to match the Number One hits of his three former cohorts, all of whom had already climbed to the top spot with albums of their own so far in 1973, but ended up having to settle for Top Ten honors only.

Billboard

9

CASH BOX

6

Record World

7

BAND ON THE RUN
PAUL McCARTNEY AND WINGS

Apple SW-3415
December 5, 1973

Band on the Run/Jet/Bluebird/Mrs. Vanderbilt/Let Me Roll It/Mamunia/ No Words/Helen Wheels/Picasso's Last Words (Drink to Me)/Nineteen Hundred and Eighty-Five

Sliced down to just three members (Paul, Linda, and Denny Laine), Wings produced their finest album to date. BAND ON THE RUN was a very tight, strong, and motivated work. Every track on the album succeeded, and even resulted in McCartney's first twelve-incher to give birth to three separate singles. ("Helen Wheels," "Jet," and "Band on the Run"—though in fact, "Helen Wheels" was actually *added* to the American version of the album after it had become a Top Ten hit.) Critically acclaimed, the album would serve as the measure to which Paul's future solo work would be judged. On the radio, airplay was extremely heavy for virtually every track.

Response was slow in building, as it took nearly six months of just hanging inside the Top Ten before it finally began to rise to the top spot on the charts, a feat which it then went on to achieve on three independent occasions, another Beatle and ex-Beatle first in the United States.

Billboard

CASH BOX

Record World

WALLS AND BRIDGES
JOHN LENNON

Apple SW-3416
September 26, 1974

**Going Down on Love/Whatever Gets
You Thru the Night/Old Dirt Road/
What You Got/Bless You/Scared/#9
Dream/Surprise, Surprise (Sweet Bird
of Paradox)/Steel and Glass/Beef
Jerky/Nobody Loves You (When You're
Down and Out)/Ya Ya**

Following another year of personal pain and confusion, John temporarily shelved the rock 'n' roll oldies project on which he had been working, and issued WALLS AND BRIDGES instead. The critics quickly divided between those who felt John had returned to the top-notch form of IMAGINE and those who thought that this album was merely OK, on a par with MIND GAMES.

Radio airplay was fairly heavy for this album, primarily for the two Top Ten hit singles it produced ("Whatever Gets You Thru the Night" and "#9 Dream"). The charts were unanimous in their Number One awards.

Billboard
☆ 1

CASH BOX
① 1

Record World
1

GOODNIGHT VIENNA
RINGO STARR

Apple SW-3417
November 18, 1974

Goodnight Vienna/Occapella/Oo-Wee/Husbands and Wives/Snook-eroo/All by Myself/Call Me/No No Song/Only You/Easy for Me/Goodnight Vienna (reprise)

Ringo teamed with producer Richard Perry once more for almost a carbon copy of RINGO, but GOODNIGHT VIENNA was not quite as strong, either in song selection or overall atmosphere. Still, it was a very enjoyable album, and did contain gems like John Lennon's title song, "Goodnight Vienna," the odd-sounding but endearing "Only You," and the hilarious novelty "No No Song"—all of which were served up as singles.

Radio airplay was fairly heavy for this album, which was vying with George's DARK HORSE on the Christmas market. Three hit singles were again pulled off the album, with the first two doing extremely well, but with the third (Lennon's title track) somehow failing to click, much to everyone's surprise. The album was a solid Top Ten hit, with *Record World* giving it Top Five status.

Billboard

8

CASH BOX

8

Record World

5

DARK HORSE
GEORGE HARRISON

Apple SMAS-3418
December 9, 1974 (December 2, 1974)

Hari's on Tour (Express)/Simply Shady/So Sad/Bye Bye Love/Maya Love/Ding Dong; Ding Dong/Dark Horse/Far East Man/It Is He (Jai Sri Krishna)

In late 1974, George became the first ex-Beatle to tour the United States. In preparing for the tour, George decided it was also time to record a new album, but unfortunately, he had rehearsed so hard for the tour that his voice had become totally hoarse. Rather than cancel the tour and hold back on the album, George went ahead and quickly recorded the songs, then dashed off on tour.

Critics, and a good number of the public, wished he had waited on both attempts until his voice was restored. The album was roundly panned, and it was clearly George's turn to fall from grace. Radio response was almost as cold as the critical reaction, while the record stalled at the No. 4 position on all three charts.

Billboard

4

CASH BOX

4

Record World

4

ROCK 'N' ROLL
JOHN LENNON

Apple SK-3419
February 17, 1975

Be-Bop-A-Lula/Stand by Me//Ready
Teddy/Rip It Up// You Can't Catch Me/
Ain't That a Shame/Do You Want to
Dance/Sweet Little Sixteen/Slippin'
and Slidin'/Peggy Sue//Bring It On
Home to Me/Send Me Some Lovin'//
Bony Moronie/Ya Ya/Just Because

John decided to pay homage to his roots by covering some of his all-time favorite rock 'n' roll tunes, many of which he performed remarkably like the originals, and which were greeted most enthusiastically by both the critics and the public. Certainly there was no denying John's vocal range as he belted out some of his strongest singing ever on this record.

ROCK 'N' ROLL had a unique history of its own, having been started in 1973 (under the title OLDIES BUT MOLDIES), then suddenly stopped, then abandoned, then restarted and finally completed in late 1974 (in the meantime, a second title, LOOK BACK, had been reported). In addition, ROCK 'N' ROLL's own spring 1975 release date had to be advanced when an unauthorized version of the album appeared in early 1975 (see ROOTS, Appendix I).

ROCK 'N' ROLL would mark the last new recordings by John to be issued before his "retirement" later in the year. The charts settled for Top Ten status, while airplay varied, but mostly centered on the Top Twenty single, "Stand By Me." A second single ("Slippin' and Slidin' "/"Ain't That a Shame," Apple 1883) was sent to radio stations but never released.

Billboard

6

CASH BOX

6

Record World

4

VENUS AND MARS
WINGS

Capitol SMAS-11419
May 27, 1975

Venus and Mars/Rock Show/Love in Song/You Gave Me the Answer/Megneto and Titanium Man/Letting Go/Venus and Mars (reprise)/Spirits of Ancient Egypt/Medicine Jar/Call Me Back Again/Listen to What the Man Said/Treat Her Gently/Lonely Old People/Crossroads Theme

Wings' follow-up to BAND ON THE RUN was noted at the time as not being quite as strong, but was nonetheless warmly received. It was certainly a very fine album in its own right, as evidenced by the fact that almost all of it was included in Wings' live act for the 1975–1976 world tour.

Mostly recorded in New Orleans, the album carried that flavor in several spots (although one song, "My Carnival," written about the Mardi Gras, was recorded but not included on the final album). Once again for Wings no fewer than three singles ("Listen to What the Man Said," "Letting Go," and "Venus and Mars/Rock Show") were extracted, though with decidedly less success—owing more to the uncertain and changing record-buying tastes of the mid-seventies than to any shortcomings of the songs themselves. Radio airplay was very heavy in all markets and the charts all agreed on its Number One honors.

Billboard

1

CASH BOX

1

Record World

1

EXTRA TEXTURE (READ ALL ABOUT IT)
GEORGE HARRISON

Apple SW-3420
September 22, 1975 (September 26, 1975)

You/The Answer's at the End/This Guitar (Can't Keep from Crying)/ Ooh Baby (You Know That I Love You)/ World of Stone/A Bit More of You/ Can't Stop Thinking About You/Tired of Midnight Blue/Grey Cloudy Lies/His Name Is Legs (Ladies & Gentlemen)

Nine months after his heavily troubled DARK HORSE album and tour, George returned in seemingly good spirits, enough so to let the Harrison sense of humor shine through not only the album's final title, EXTRA TEXTURE (READ ALL ABOUT IT), but in what was originally to have been the title, OHNOTHIMAGEN.

Although George's voice had returned, the material was once again on the weak side, though critics at the time gave the album some decidedly good reviews. Except for the single, "You," airplay was fairly light, though it sold just enough to make the Top Ten on all three charts.

Billboard

8

CASH BOX

9

Record World

9

SHAVED FISH
JOHN LENNON

Apple SW-3421
October 24, 1975 (October 22, 1975)

Give Peace a Chance/Cold Turkey/
Instant Karma/Power to the People/
Mother/Woman Is the Nigger of the
World/Imagine/Whatever Gets You
Thru the Night/Mind Games/#9
Dream//Happy Xmas (War Is Over)/
Give Peace a Chance

Most called this album John's "greatest hits," but what some people failed to realize was that this was merely a collection of all of John's solo singles, some of which were unavailable on his albums, and denoted as such by the cover's promotional sticker, which subtitled the record "Collectable Lennon."

Released just in time for Christmas, this package failed to sell anywhere near the mark expected, just falling short of the Top Ten on *Billboard,* while barely making and barely missing the Top Twenty on the other two charts.

Billboard

12

CASH BOX

19

Record World

21

BLAST FROM YOUR PAST
RINGO STARR

Apple SW-3422
November 20, 1975

You're Sixteen/No No Song/It Don't
Come Easy/Photograph/Back Off
Boogaloo/Only You/Beaucoups Of
Blues/Oh My My/Early 1970/ I'm the
Greatest

The bigger they are, the harder they fall. Surely a "greatest hits" album featuring all of Ringo's early seventies chart-topping singles was just what was needed at Christmastime 1975, right? Wrong! Despite all that it had going for it, this album clearly demonstrated how quickly the record business changes. The songs on this album had all topped the charts within the past four years or less, yet the album failed to sell anywhere near what was expected and certainly deserved.

For anyone wishing to sample Ringo's "greatest hits," it is still a marvelous collection. Why it wasn't in 1975 is still a deep mystery. One problem though was the lack of airplay, as all the songs were "oldies" at the time. Incidentally, this was the very last Apple Records album ever to be released.

Billboard
★ 30

CASH BOX
(40)

Record World
[64]

WINGS AT THE SPEED OF SOUND
WINGS

Capitol SW-11525
March 25, 1976 (March 23, 1976)

Let 'Em In/The Note You Never Wrote/ She's My Baby/Beware My Love/Wino Junko/Silly Love Songs/Cook of the House/Time to Hide/Must Do Something About It/San Ferry Anne/Warm and Beautiful

WINGS AT THE SPEED OF SOUND was released just prior to the group's premiere tour of the United States in the spring of 1976, and a very obvious attempt on Paul's part to make this a much more group-oriented effort than any previous Wings album, with vocals from all members of the group included.

Critical response was generally favorable as a result, while the public sent sales soaring—a direct consequence of the fact that the band was on tour. It was also spirited along by two chart-topping singles ("Silly Love Songs" and "Let 'Em In"), and airplay was fairly heavy for several tracks, notably even for most of the non-McCartney-sung tunes. Wings enjoyed their fourth consecutive Number One album on all three charts.

Billboard

☆ 1

CASH BOX

(1)

Record World

| 1 |

ROCK 'N' ROLL MUSIC
THE BEATLES

Capitol SKBO-11537
June 7, 1976 (June 11, 1976)

Twist and Shout/I Saw Her Standing There/You Can't Do That/I Wanna Be Your Man/I Call Your Name/Boys/Long Tall Sally/Rock and Roll Music/Slow Down//Kansas City/Hey Hey Hey Hey//Money/Bad Boy/Matchbox/Roll Over Beethoven/Dizzy Miss Lizzie/Anytime at All/Drive My Car/Everybody's Trying to Be My Baby/The Night Before/I'm Down/Revolution/Back in the U.S.S.R./Helter Skelter/Taxman/Got to Get You Into My Life/Hey Bulldog/Birthday/Get Back

Three years after the last Beatles reissue product, Capitol decided it was time again to repackage some more *classic* Beatles tunes and serve them up in a two-record set. The thought that Paul McCartney would be touring the United States at the time of this album's release might also have occurred to Capitol.

For this effort, Capitol chose a representation of the group's hardest-rocking numbers, and titled the set after one of them, ROCK 'N' ROLL MUSIC. John Lennon offered to design a cover but was turned down, and instead, a ridiculous cover featuring drawings of the Beatles on the outside and fifties memorabilia on the inside was put together—a cover horrible enough for Ringo publicly to condemn it.

Even so, the album shot to the top, being stopped only by the Wings' album that already occupied the Number One position. Radio airplay of these old Beatles tunes sharply increased, and along with Paul's tour helped to spur another wave of renewed Beatlemania that lasted most of the summer.

Billboard

2

CASH BOX

4

Record World

2

RINGO'S ROTOGRAVURE
RINGO STARR

Atlantic SD-18193
September 27, 1976

A Dose of Rock'n'Roll/Hey Baby/Pure Gold/Cryin'/You Don't Know Me at All/Cookin' (In the Kitchen of Love)/I'll Still Love You/This Be Called a Song/Las Brisas/Lady Gaye/Spooky Weirdness

Although he had a new record label (Atlantic) and a new producer (Arif Mardin), Ringo tried playing it safe, and attempted another album in the prototype RINGO mold. However, this format had become rather obvious and a bit boring—decidedly the weakest of the three rock albums thus far from Mr. Starr in the seventies.

RINGO'S ROTOGRAVURE failed to gain even a hint of the success that the two previous outings had so richly enjoyed. Even the use of songs and performances from each of the other three former Beatles failed to help very much. Only two singles were tried, with the first ("A Dose of Rock 'n' Roll") barely skirting the Top Thirty, and the second ("Hey Baby") hardly skipping in and out of the charts at all. Radio airplay was very light.

Billboard

28

CASH BOX

56

Record World

45

THE BEST OF GEORGE HARRISON
GEORGE HARRISON (and THE BEATLES)

Capitol ST-11578
November 8, 1976

Something/If I Needed Someone/Here Comes the Sun/Taxman/Think for Yourself/For You Blue/ While My Guitar Gently Weeps (The Beatles)/My Sweet Lord/Give Me Love (Give Me Peace on Earth)/You/Bangla Desh/Dark Horse/ What Is Life (Harrison)

Just in time for Christmas, Capitol took action on its option to put together a *greatest hits* package of George Harrison tracks. Although the release date would coincide with the release of an album of new material, George even offered to help select the tracks and running order for the Capitol package. Amazingly, Capitol once again turned down an ex-Beatle, and instead came up with a selection of songs that featured George's solo singles on one side, and his songs written and performed with the Beatles on the other. In effect, Capitol was saying that Harrison simply hadn't produced enough material on his own worthy of "greatest hits" status. The fact that half of this album is really the Beatles hurt and embarrassed George a great deal.

Curiously, and as with all the ex-Beatle solo *greatest hits* albums, this one failed to sell anything close to expectations, barely rising to the Top Thirty level.

Billboard

31

CASH BOX

29

Record World

33

THIRTY THREE & 1/3
GEORGE HARRISON

Dark Horse DH-3005
November 24, 1976

Woman Don't You Cry for Me/Dear One/Beautiful Girl/This Song/See Yourself/It's What You Value/True Love/Pure Smokey/Crackerbox Palace/Learning How to Love You

Competing as it was for Christmas sales against his own BEST OF album, George must have been pleased with the public's response and critical reaction to THIRTY THREE & 1/3, which arrived on the scene soon after the Capitol album hit the stores. THIRTY THREE & 1/3 was uptempo and high spirited, featuring some nice electric guitar playing by George, and some nice horn arrangements by co-producer Tom Scott.

For many, this was George's best effort in quite some time. Radio airplay was fair to good, pushed along mainly by two hit singles ("This Song" and "Crackerbox Palace"), and the album just missed making the Top Ten.

Billboard

11

CASH BOX

15

Record World

14

WINGS OVER AMERICA
WINGS

Capitol SWCO-11593
December 10, 1976

Venus and Mars/Rock Show/Jet//Let Me Roll It/Spirits of Ancient Egypt/ Medicine Jar/Maybe I'm Amazed/Call Me Back Again/Lady Madonna/The Long and Winding Road/Live and Let Die/Picasso's Last Words/Richard Corey/Bluebird/I've Just Seen a Face/ Blackbird/Yesterday/You Gave Me the Answer/Magneto and Titanium Man/Go Now/My Love/Listen to What the Man Said/Let 'Em In/Time to Hide/Silly Love Songs/Beware My Love/Letting Go/Band on the Run/Hi Hi Hi/Soily

The first official live recordings of Paul and Wings since 1973's B-side; "The Mess," almost made for a *"McCartney's Greatest Hits—Live!"* package. This three-record set of the entire thirty-song show featured on the 1976 Wings Over America leg of the Wings Over the World tour was released just in time for Christmas. With five Beatles songs thrown in for good measure, who could resist? This package was especially irresistible because there was no doubt that many of the songs sounded infinitely superior "live" than they had in their original studio forms.

The critics were very favorable in their evaluations of this offering, and even with its triple-set price tag it still sold well enough to top the chart at *Billboard,* and almost do the same on *Cash Box* and *Record World.* Radio airplay was surprisingly light, although extremely heavy sales were experienced.

Billboard

1

CASH BOX
②
2

Record World
3

211

THE BEATLES AT THE HOLLYWOOD BOWL
THE BEATLES

Capitol SMAS-11638
May 4, 1977

Twist and Shout/She's a Woman/
Dizzy Miss Lizzie/Ticket to Ride/
Can't Buy Me Love/Things We Said
Today/Roll Over Beethoven/Boys/A
Hard Day's Night/ Help!/All My
Loving/She Loves You/Long Tall Sally

After many years of debate, rumor, speculation, and waiting, Capitol finally released an official *live* Beatles album. Capitol meshed together two separate recordings of the Beatles at the Hollywood Bowl, one made in 1964 and the other in 1965, to simulate a single-concert performance, rather than issue a double-album set featuring both complete concerts. In any case, better late than never, as this album will serve as a document of that initial period of frenzied Beatlemania in the United States and around the world. Interesting also to note is that Apple reportedly considered releasing this album in 1971 but never followed through.

Radio airplay was fair to mildly good, depending on the market, while only *Record World* seemed to disagree with the almost-chart-topping positions given by *Billboard* and *Cash Box*.

Billboard

☆ 2

CASH BOX

③

Record World

| 7 |

LIVE AT THE STAR CLUB IN HAMBURG, GERMANY, 1962
THE BEATLES

Atlantic/Lingasong LS-2-7001
June 13, 1977

THE BEATLES Live! at the Star-Club in Hamburg, Germany; 1962.

I'm Gonna Sit Right Down and Cry (Over You)/Roll Over Beethoven/Hippy Hippy Shake/Sweet Little Sixteen/Lend Me Your Comb/Your Feet's Too Big/Where Have You Been All My Life/Mr. Moonlight/A Taste of Honey/Besame Mucho/Till There Was You//Kansas City/Hey Hey Hey Hey//Nothin' Shakin' (But the Leaves on the Trees)/To Know Her Is to Love Her/Little Queenie/Falling in Love Again/Sheila/Be-Bop-A-Lula/Hallelujah, I Love Her So/Red Sails in the Sunset/Everybody's Trying to Be My Baby/Matchbox/I'm Talking About You/Shimmy Shake/Long Tall Sally/I Remember You

One month after Capitol's live album, Atlantic/Lingasong released this also-much-awaited live album, despite some last minute legal maneuvers by the Beatles to try to stop the record from coming out. Their court bid failed, and almost fifteen years after it had been recorded, Beatles fans had a chance to hear the group truly as never before, performing live on stage in Hamburg, Germany, their legendary training ground in the early sixties before rising to fame.

The raw excitement and high energy displayed in this double set provided a sharp contrast to the almost lethargic performances during the heights of Beatlemania featured on the Capitol live album. Unfortunately, the sound quality left a lot to be desired, but even so, this was truly a historic and valuable discovery, and should have been better received by the public than it was. Limited radio exposure owed largely to the "sound quality" excuse, though compared with many of the punk rock records surfacing at the time, this seemed a questionable justification. For *pure* rock 'n' roll Beatles, this recording couldn't be beat.

Billboard ☆ 111   **CASH BOX** 183   **Record World** 165

213

RINGO THE 4th
RINGO STARR

Atlantic SD-19108
September 26, 1977

Drowning in the Sea of Love/Tango All Night/Wings/Gave It All Up/Out on the Streets/Can She Do It Like She Dances/Sneaking Sally Through the Alley/It's No Secret/Gypsies in Flight/Simple Love Song

One has to wonder if the cover photo for this record was taken after Ringo had heard the test pressing. This album was such a disappointment for a former Beatle that it was almost enough to consider seriously whether Ringo might actually be sticking the sword into himself as the warranted punishment for even bothering to release this mess.

The songs on RINGO THE 4th were designed for a Monte Carlo casino lounge act, and perhaps in that setting they might have worked. In fact, the promotional film for "Drowning in the Sea of Love" featured that exact setting. However, as a vehicle for a pop star, even in the disco-oriented late seventies, this collection didn't hold its own even on those merits. A pair of singles ("Wings" and "Drowning in the Sea of Love") both failed to gain any airplay, and the entire effort stands as one of the worst album chart players ever in all Beatles history.

Billboard
162

CASH BOX
194

Record World
178

LOVE SONGS
THE BEATLES

Capitol SKBL-11711
October 21, 1977 (October 24, 1977)

Yesterday/I'll Follow the Sun/I Need You/Girl/In My Life/Words of Love/Here, There and Everywhere/Something/And I Love Her/If I Fell/I'll Be Back/Tell Me What You See/Yes It Is/Michelle/It's Only Love/You're Gonna Lose That Girl/Every Little Thing/For No One/She's Leaving Home/ The Long and Winding Road/This Boy/Norwegian Wood (This Bird Has Flown)/You've Got to Hide Your Love Away/I Will/P.S. I Love You

Capitol decided it was time to try another two-record repackage of vintage Beatles material, this time out selecting the group's softer and more tender side, appropriately though unimaginatively titled LOVE SONGS, and packaged in a simulated leather jacket with a gold embossed (and slightly retouched) photo of the Beatles on the cover, complete with parchment paper lyric book. Who could resist this perfect Christmas gift, released by chance just in time to take care of one's holiday needs.

For some reason, this set did not sell, and certainly came nowhere near the success ROCK 'N' ROLL MUSIC had enjoyed. Perhaps the fans were foreseeing future Capitol repackages (The Beatles DRUG SONGS, etc.) and were telling the company that in the future they had better raid the vaults for material that was not already on its fourth, fifth, and sixth go-rounds.

Billboard
★ 24

CASH BOX
(28)

Record World
| 36 |

LONDON TOWN
WINGS

Capitol SW-11777
March 31, 1978

London Town/Cafe on the Left Bank/
I'm Carrying//Backwards Traveller/
Cuff Link//Children Children/Girl-
friend/I've Had Enough/With a Little
Luck/Famous Groupies/Deliver Your
Children/Name and Address/Don't Let
It Bring You Down/Morse Moose and
the Grey Goose

Once again clipped to just Paul, Linda, and Denny Laine for most of the album, Wings' first studio release in almost two years was a very ambitious effort in terms of the amount of tracks offered, but a bit less rewarding and perhaps too laid-back than was hoped for by most listeners at the time. Still, the album featured a wide range of styles and sounds, owing not only to the personnel changes but to the fact that the album was recorded in a variety of locations, most notably upon a chartered yacht in the Caribbean.

Critical response ranged from fair at best, to downright harsh. Radio airplay however was good, with heavy airing for at least two ("With a Little Luck" and "I've Had Enough") of the album's three ("London Town" being the third) hit singles. On the charts, LONDON TOWN stopped just short of the top spot.

Billboard

☆ 2

CASH BOX

(2)

Record World

[2]

BAD BOY
RINGO STARR

Portrait JR-35378
April 21, 1978

Who Needs a Heart/Bad Boy/Lipstick
Traces/Heart on My Sleeve/Where Did
Our Love Go/Hard Times/Tonight/
Monkey See Monkey Do/Old Time
Relovin'/A Man Like Me

Ringo tried to bounce back in the spring of 1978 with a new album and a TV special. Unfortunately, both faltered, though they deserved to be received a bit more enthusiastically. BAD BOY had much more life to it than the empty RINGO THE 4th which preceded it, and, in fact, contained some of Ringo's best songs in many a year ("Hard Times," "Who Needs a Heart," "Heart on My Sleeve"). However, the remainder of tunes were as dreadful and meaningless as ever. Hearing Ringo do a disco cover version of the Supremes' "Where Did Our Love Go" was indeed a major letdown.

A pair of singles failed to go anywhere, and radio airplay was zip. The chart reflected a slight rise above RINGO THE 4th levels, but it was still another major disappointment for the former Beatle who had prospered so well on his own in the early seventies. Apparently the charm had worn off. Hard times indeed.

129

CASH BOX

97

Record World

144

THE BEATLES TAPES
David Wigg interviews THE BEATLES

P.B.R. International 7005/7006
1978

(Interviews) John Lennon and Yoko Ono — June 1969/Paul McCartney — March 1970/George Harrison — September 1969/Ringo Starr — December 1968/ Ringo Starr — December 1973/(additional instrumental tracks by Martyn Ford and orchestra are interspersed between segments)

More than two years after this album had been issued in the UK and heavily imported into the United States, P.B.R. International finally gave this record the proper American release.

Containing interviews with each of the four Beatles recorded at various times between 1968 and 1973, as well as a book of photographs, this album was unable to generate much in the way of sales even though pressed on blue vinyl, apparently to coincide with Capitol's colored-vinyl reissues at the time. Most fans who would ever want THE BEATLES TAPES had long ago purchased the import version on Polydor. The album also suffered from poor distribution, resulting in general unavailability, and even in the public's ignorance of its existence in many areas of the nation.

BEATLE TALK
Red Robinson interviews THE BEATLES

Great Northwest Music Co. GWC-4007
November 15, 1978

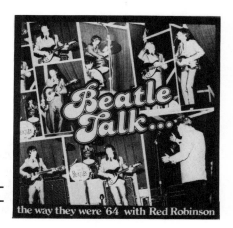

**(Interviews) Vancouver, Canada —
August 1964/Seattle, Washington —
August 1966**

Almost simultaneously with THE BEATLES TAPES came this odd release, an interview album that featured excerpts from the Beatles' press conference in Vancouver, Canada, in 1964, and another in Seattle in 1966.

The liner notes went to great trouble to point out that the tapes used were from the private collection of Red Robinson (though both interviews had been available for many years on a number of bootlegs), that the album contained no music by the Beatles, that it was only a talking record, and that it was not a Capitol Records product.

As with THE BEATLES TAPES, BEATLES TALK failed to stir much activity, at least not enough to gain any airplay or chart action, and was a bit hard to come by in many parts of the country.

WINGS GREATEST
WINGS

Capitol SOO-11905
November 22, 1978

Another Day/Silly Love Songs/Live
and Let Die/Junior's Farm/With a Little
Luck/Band on the Run//Uncle Albert/
Admiral Halsey//Hi Hi Hi/Let 'Em In/
My Love/Jet/Mull of Kintyre

Part Four of the great mystery of the seventies: Paul's solo "greatest hits" album followed the example set by those of the other three Beatles and failed to sell anything like what was most certainly expected. Despite the plethora of Number One and Top Ten hits included on this disc, released just in time for the 1978 holiday gift-giving season, WINGS GREATEST fell way short at the accountant's ledger. Even the inclusion of several songs previously only available as singles was unable to enlist sizable sales.

Radio airplay was virtually non-existent, while on the charts the album barely scratched near the Top Twenty. By the way, this was Paul's last album for Capitol Records in the United States. After fifteen years with EMI/Capitol in America, he was moving on to Columbia Records.

Billboard

29

CASH BOX

21

Record World

23

GEORGE HARRISON
GEORGE HARRISON

Dark Horse DHK-3255
February 14, 1979

Love Comes to Everyone/Not Guilty/
Here Comes the Moon/Soft-Hearted
Hana/Blow Away/Faster/Dark Sweet
Lady/Your Love Is Forever/Soft
Touch/If You Believe

After another two-year-plus wait, the public was finally offered the follow-up to 1976's THIRTY THREE & 1/3. The music on GEORGE HARRISON was softer than its predecessor's, but the acoustic-guitar-led numbers and laid-back electric guitar tunes worked rather well, and a good number of both critics and the general audience felt that George had come up with his best album since ALL THINGS MUST PASS.

Radio airplay was fair to good, and undoubtedly George's strongest showing in some time, though George came up short of the Top Ten on all three charts.

  Billboard
☆ 14

CASH BOX
(12)

Record World
[17]

BACK TO THE EGG
WINGS

Columbia FC-36057
May 24, 1979

Reception/Getting Closer/We're Open Tonight/Spin It On/Again and Again and Again/Old Siam, Sir/Arrow Through Me/Rockestra Theme/To You//After the Ball/Million Miles// Winter Rose/Love Awake//The Broadcast/So Glad to See You Here/ Baby's Request

Paul's first album for Columbia (North America only) featured a new Wings line-up, potentially the strongest one yet. Although featuring some of Wings' roughest rockers in a number of years, thanks in part to co-producer Chris Thomas, BACK TO THE EGG failed to endear itself to many critics, while the vast public seemed only marginally approving of it. Too bad, as it was a much better record than it was given credit for.

Airplay was only moderate at best, while the charts stalled it out on the wrong end of the Top Ten.

Billboard

8

CASH BOX

⑦

Record World

7

RARITIES
THE BEATLES

Capitol SHAL-12060
March 24, 1980

Love Me Do/Misery/There's a Place/
Sie Liebt Dich/And I Love Her/Help!/
I'm Only Sleeping/I Am the Walrus/
Penny Lane/Helter Skelter/Don't Pass
Me By/The Inner Light/Across the
Universe/You Know My Name (Look Up
My Number)/Sgt. Pepper Inner Groove

Capitol's first repackage effort since 1977's LOVE SONGS met with good critical acclaim and public response. RARITIES brought together slightly odd versions and mixes of a dozen or so previously released tracks, most of which had not been included on American albums before. The collection was especially interesting and valuable to Beatles fans and collectors, but was appealing as well to the general record-buying public.

Capitol created some added sales zest by including a new and improved full-sized version of the infamous "Butcher" photo, though it was featured on the inside of the cover. Had it been touted on the front of the album it probably would have gained a million impulse sales. RARITIES still managed to perform better than Capitol had thought it would, doing decidedly better than LOVE SONGS, though by no means doing as well as a real album of *true rarities* could. Radio airplay was devoted mostly to the songs from the group's later period, on side two.

Billboard

21

CASH BOX

20

Record World

26

McCARTNEY II
PAUL McCARTNEY

Columbia FC-36511
May 21, 1980

Coming Up/Temporary Secretary/On the Way/Waterfalls/Nobody Knows/Front Parlour/Summer Day Song/Frozen Jap/Bogey Music/Darkroom/One of These Days

After BACK TO THE EGG, Paul recorded an album of songs completely by himself, never intending them for general release. After playing tapes of the tracks to friends, he was urged to consider putting them out. Upon returning to England after his "adventure" in Japan, he decided to go ahead and issue the first completely solo non-Wings McCartney album in a full decade.

Although an impressive musical one-man show, as was his first solo album, McCARTNEY II suffered slightly because of Paul's having traded in his guitar and drums (which dominated McCARTNEY) for electronic organs, synthesizers, speeded-up vocal tricks, and other assorted gimmicks.

Two singles ("Coming Up" and "Waterfalls") were pulled from the package, although it was the live B-side of the first that was the actual smash hit. In fact, due to consumer demands, the initial pressing of the album included a free one-sided single of the live version of "Coming Up." Except for this track, radio airplay for the remainder of the album was only fair. Even so, it sold well enough to place near the top of the charts.

Billboard

☆ 3

CASH BOX

(3)

Record World

[3]

ROCK 'N' ROLL MUSIC—VOLUME 1
THE BEATLES

Capitol SN-16020
October 1980

Twist and Shout/I Saw Her Standing
There/You Can't Do That/I Wanna Be
Your Man/I Call Your Name/Boys/
Long Tall Sally/Rock and Roll Music/
Slow Down//Kansas City/Hey Hey
Hey Hey//Money/Bad Boy/Match-
box/Roll Over Beethoven

Capitol issued its first Beatles albums on its budget line by deleting the 1976 ROCK 'N' ROLL MUSIC double album and splitting it into two separate single albums. In addition, Capitol designed entirely new covers for the twin pair, which were designated VOLUME ONE and VOLUME TWO.

These would have been mentioned strictly in the reissue section of this book except that, due to the Lennon death and the public's great rush to buy up as many Lennon and Beatles albums as possible, both of these reissue albums sold well enough to make the charts, something they most assuredly would not have done otherwise. Nonetheless, the fact remains that they did chart, and because of their status as something other than just a typical reissue (they were actually two "new" single albums), they have been included here.

CASH BOX

Record World

☆ — (—) 134

ROCK 'N' ROLL MUSIC—VOLUME 2
THE BEATLES

Capitol SN-16021
October 1980

Dizzy Miss Lizzie/Anytime at All/ Drive My Car/Everybody's Trying to Be My Baby/The Night Before/I'm Down/Revolution/Back in the U.S.S.R./Helter Skelter/Taxman/Got to Get You Into My Life/Hey Bulldog/ Birthday/Get Back

This was the second volume of the ROCK 'N' ROLL MUSIC double album reissued as two separate budget-line releases. As for the same reasons noted for VOLUME ONE, this album also quite unexpectedly entered the charts.

Billboard
☆

CASH BOX
⊖

Record World
137

DOUBLE FANTASY
JOHN LENNON AND YOKO ONO

Geffen GHS-2001
November 17, 1980

(Just Like) Starting Over/Kiss Kiss Kiss/Clean-up Time/Give Me Something/I'm Losing You/I'm Moving On/Beautiful Boy (Darling Boy)/Watching the Wheels/I'm Your Angel/Woman/Beautiful Boys/Dear Yoko/Every Man Has a Woman Who Loves Him/Hard Times Are Over

The Lennons' long-awaited and much-anticipated return from their five-year "retirement" to the world of rock music took place in the form of a new album together, DOUBLE FANTASY, on which the couple each contributed seven numbers. The result was presented in an almost dialogue format, as John's songs alternated with Yoko's, in a tone and setting where the central message was the same as it had always been: *love*. DOUBLE FANTASY found John and Yoko sharing their love for one another, for their child, and for everyone.

The album had just entered the charts, and was about to make its way into the Top Ten, when the untimely events of December 8 occurred. In its wake, stores immediately sold out of DOUBLE FANTASY (not only nationwide, but worldwide as well), and not surprisingly it rose to the top of the charts, while airplay for much of the album was at extremely heavy saturation levels.

THE McCARTNEY INTERVIEW
PAUL McCARTNEY

Columbia PC-36987 (Limited Edition)
December 4, 1980

THE McCARTNEY INTERVIEW originally appeared as a special promotional-use-only double album (Columbia A2S-821) shortly after the release in May of McCARTNEY II. But it was so well received by radio stations and listeners that public demand and interest for the record finally led to this single-album release. (Not to worry, the second record of the double-album set only contained edited or excerpted answers of the interview featured on record one, and the commercially issued single album was identical to record one.)

Columbia planned an initial Limited Edition run of 10,000, but this was upped to 57,000 for this budget-line release. Radio airplay had already come in the spring and summer, but the public's interest in a new McCartney record led to a minor rush, and enough copies were sold to allow it to slip onto the charts.

Billboard

158

CASH BOX

⊖

Record World

141

CONCERTS FOR THE PEOPLE OF KAMPUCHEA
Various artists featuring PAUL McCARTNEY AND WINGS

Atlantic SD 2 7005
March 30, 1981

Got to Get You Into My Life/Every Night/Coming Up (Wings)/Lucille/Let It Be/Rockestra Theme (Rockestra)/ (additional tracks featuring The Who, The Pretenders, Queen, Elvis Costello and the Attractions, Rockpile, Ian Dury and the Blockheads, The Clash, The Specials)

In December 1979, a series of benefit concerts was held in London to raise money for the people of Kampuchea (formerly Cambodia). Almost a year and a half later, an album containing highlights of those concerts was finally released.

Performing on the last night (December 29) was Paul and Wings. Their set was followed by a special added bonus performance by most of the members of Rockestra, the all-star session ensemble from BACK TO THE EGG. Taking up all of side four, Wings are showcased with three numbers, followed by three tracks from Wings and Rockestra. Included are live versions of "Let It Be" and "Got to Get You Into My Life."

Despite featuring entire sides by Wings and The Who, as well as other current top-draw acts the album failed ever to gain any real momentum or interest. Certainly Atlantic had counted on enough Wings and Who fans alone to help pace sales, but they never materialized. Radio airplay was only fair to good, while the chart action was disappointing considering the potential of this two-disc set.

Billboard

⭐ 36

CASH BOX

(31)

Record World

[31]

SOMEWHERE IN ENGLAND
GEORGE HARRISON

Dark Horse DHK 3492
June 1, 1981

Hong Kong Blues/Writing's on the Wall/ Flying Hour/Lay His Head/Unconsciousness Rules/Sat Singing/Life Itself/Tears of the World/Baltimore Oriole/Save the World (Revised/released version) Blood from a Clone/ Unconsciousness Rules/Life Itself/All Those Years Ago/Baltimore Oriole/Teardrops/That Which I Have Lost/ Writing's on the Wall/Hong Kong Blues/Save the World

SOMEWHERE IN ENGLAND was originally completed and scheduled for release in October 1980. However, Warner Brothers decided at the last moment to withhold the album from release, and requested that George "rework" it a bit. Subsequently, four of the album's ten tracks were dropped ("Tears of the World," "Lay His Head," "Flying Hour," and "Sat Singing") and replaced with four new songs ("All Those Years Ago," "Teardrops," "Blood from a Clone," and "That Which I Have Lost"). In addition, the original cover artwork was scrapped and a new jacket was substituted.

Initial interest in the album was quite high, especially since it had once again been more than two years since George's last release. Despite its lengthy genesis, the final result was at least pleasant enough for many critics to reward George with passing grades. Radio airplay, except for the almost chart-topping "All Those Years Ago," was unfairly minimal for the remainder of the album. Hence, it managed its quick rise to within just a hair of the Top Ten on all three charts on the strength of sales alone.

Billboard

11

CASH BOX

11

Record World

11

STOP AND SMELL THE ROSES
RINGO STARR

Boardwalk NB1-33246
October 27, 1981 (October 23, 1981)

Private Property/Wrack My Brain/
Drumming Is My Madness/Attention/
Stop and Take the Time to Smell the
Roses/Dead Giveaway/You Belong to
Me/Sure to Fall/Nice Way/Back Off
Boogaloo

STOP AND SMELL THE ROSES became the first Ringo Starr album to be released in more than three and a half years. The bulk of the tracks had originally been recorded in mid-1980, and the album was originally scheduled for early 1981 release under the title CAN'T FIGHT LIGHTNING. However, Ringo's sudden departure from Portrait Records in America delayed the release until he was signed to Boardwalk.

This album featured contributions from a host of well-known rock stars, highlighted by major contributions from fellow ex-Beatles George Harrison and Paul McCartney. Even John Lennon had been scheduled to record some new songs with Ringo early in 1981. However, in light of the tragic turn of events, Ringo chose not to include any of Lennon's tunes on the album, nor did he include the original title track, "Can't Fight Lightning," a number reportedly about his falling in love with Barbara Bach.

Nonetheless, STOP AND SMELL THE ROSES was not well received. The public seemed mixed, while the critics strongly disliked it. Airplay was virtually nil, save for the single "Wrack My Brain," and the charts showed it to be only a mild improvement over BAD BOY.

Billboard

98

CASH BOX

93

Record World

78

REEL MUSIC
THE BEATLES

Capitol SV-12199
March 22, 1982

A Hard Day's Night / I Should Have Known Better / Can't Buy Me Love / And I Love Her / Help! / You've Got to Hide Your Love Away / Ticket to Ride / Magical Mystery Tour / I Am the Walrus / Yellow Submarine / All You Need Is Love / Let It Be / Get Back / The Long and Winding Road

Capitol's first Beatles compilation in two years found the company returning to recycling existing material for the umpteenth time, rather than delving into the vaults and producing something of real interest and value. This time out the theme chosen was "movie songs," hence the clever title REEL MUSIC.

Critics found the album's cover even worse, and noted it was so poorly conceived and executed that it was doubtful whether it appealed to anyone over the age of six. In fact, the art was so atrociously bad, some of the drawings of the group made it difficult, if not nearly impossible, to determine which Beatle was supposedly which. If the former Beatles had been outraged at the cover art for ROCK'N'ROLL MUSIC, one could only imagine their reaction to this mess. It even managed to sink below the level of slipshod design usually associated with most albums sold only via TV ads.

Plugged for its generous offering of fourteen songs and a special booklet of "rare" photos, this was merely utilized to justify a raise in the list price a dollar above normal. As for the "rare" photos, nearly all of them had been published in literally dozens of magazines and books over the years. In fact, the photos representing *Magical Mystery Tour* were quite simply the set of photos originally included in the booklet that came with that album (though after 1980, Capitol no longer packaged MAGICAL MYSTERY TOUR with its book).

Thanks in part to a fairly extensive promotional campaign, the album surprisingly sold well enough to place in the Top Twenty.

Billboard   CASH BOX   *Record World*

⭐ 19   (18) | 90* |

After the record debuted at No. 90 the week of 4/10/82, Record World ceased publication.

TUG OF WAR
PAUL McCARTNEY

Columbia TC 37462
April 26, 1982

Tug of War / Take It Away / Somebody
Who Cares / What's That You're Doing?
/ Here Today / Ballroom Dancing / The
Pound Is Sinking / Wanderlust / Get It
/ Be What You See / Dress Me Up As
a Robber / Ebony and Ivory

With the release of TUG OF WAR, Paul's first album in two years, the only real controversy surrounding it at the time was between those critics and members of the public who felt it was his best effort since BAND ON THE RUN, and those who felt it was quite simply his most musically accomplished and satisfying work ever. Re-teamed with former Beatles producer George Martin for the first time since 1973's "Live and Let Die" single, and littered throughout with superstar musicians (among them Ringo Starr, Stevie Wonder, Carl Perkins), TUG OF WAR received nearly universal praise of the highest order from everyone concerned, and apparently, that included just about "everyone," as this album immediately ascended to the top of the charts.*

CASH BOX

*Record World *ceased publication just prior to the release of this album.*

APPENDIX

I

REISSUES AND SPECIAL ITEMS OF INTEREST

This section mainly covers reissues of singles and albums that significantly differ in one or more ways from the original release. This includes deleted product that resurfaces years later, perhaps on a different label, and sometimes even under a different title with new cover or sleeve artwork.

In most cases, reissues are intended merely to serve as back-catalog product. Rather than make the material that was included on a new-deleted single or album totally unavailable, the reissue makes this oldies product obtainable once again. As a rule, and especially in the case of Beatles-related product, reissues are usually just slipped onto the market very quietly with little or no announcement or fanfare, perhaps spread out over a period of time, and therefore not promoted or expected to sell strongly enough all at once to make the charts.

The few other items of special interest included in this section deal primarily with unique and sometimes questionable Beatles-related releases not really considered ''chartable'' product for various reasons as noted.

Singles

DO YOU WANT TO KNOW A SECRET/
  Thank You Girl

Oldies 45 OL-149

PLEASE PLEASE ME/
  From Me to You

Oldies 45 OL-150

LOVE ME DO/P.S. I Love You

Oldies 45 OL-151

TWIST AND SHOUT/
  There's a Place

Oldies 45 OL-152

THE BEATLES
August 10, 1964

Vee Jay deleted the four Beatles singles they had released earlier in the year (two of which had actually appeared on Vee Jay's subsidiary label, Tollie) and reissued them on the Oldies 45 label.

TWIST AND SHOUT/
There's a Place

Capitol Starline 6061

LOVE ME DO/
P.S. I Love You

Capitol Starline 6062

PLEASE PLEASE ME/
From Me to You

Capitol Starline 6063

DO YOU WANT TO KNOW A SECRET/
Thank You Girl

Capitol Starline 6064

ROLL OVER BEETHOVEN/
Misery

Capitol Starline 6065

BOYS/
Kansas City

Capitol Starline 6066

THE BEATLES
October 11, 1965

In another move after acquiring the rights to the Vee Jay catalog of Beatles tunes, Capitol reissued the four Vee Jay/Tollie/Oldies 45 singles on their own Starline label, which featured hits of the past. Capitol also issued two "new" singles, each made up of an additional Vee Jay track coupled with an EMI selection, one of which managed to gain airplay and make the charts (see: "Boys"/"Kansas City"—October 11, 1965).

Philadelphia Freedom/
I SAW HER STANDING THERE
Elton John Band featuring JOHN LENNON
  (A-side: Elton John Band)

MCA 40364
February 24, 1975

Would you believe a single featuring John Lennon singing a live version of "I Saw Her Standing There" that sold a million copies and rose to Number One on the charts—yet one that most fans were not even aware of? In actuality, this was Elton John's new record, with the A-side, "Philadelphia Freedom" gaining all of the attention and airplay.

The B-side contained the rare Lennon gem, recorded live in concert at Madison Square Garden on November 28, 1974, during Elton's Thanksgiving concert. (Lennon and Elton also performed and recorded "Whatever Gets You Thru the Night" and "Lucy in the Sky with Diamonds" that night, but these tracks were not released until 1981.)

STAND BY ME/WOMAN IS THE NIGGER OF THE WORLD
JOHN LENNON

Capitol Starline 6244

DARK HORSE/YOU
GEORGE HARRISON

Capitol Starline 6425

April 4, 1977

In the spring of 1977, Capitol deleted two John Lennon and two George Harrison singles, paired the A-sides, and released two Starline singles in their place. This was the first Beatles product to go onto the Starline label in twelve years.

GETTING CLOSER/GOODNIGHT TONIGHT
WINGS

Columbia Hall of Fame 13-33405

MY LOVE/MAYBE I'M AMAZED
A-side: PAUL McCARTNEY AND WINGS
B-side: PAUL McCARTNEY

Columbia Hall of Fame 13-33407

UNCLE ALBERT/ADMIRAL HALSEY//JET
A-side: PAUL AND LINDA McCARTNEY
B-side: PAUL McCARTNEY AND WINGS

Columbia Hall of Fame 13-33408

BAND ON THE RUN/HELEN WHEELS
PAUL McCARTNEY AND WINGS

Columbia Hall of Fame 13-33409

December 4, 1980

Almost two years after Paul joined Columbia, the label began reissuing his deleted Capitol/Apple singles. This was done by combining the A-sides of some of Paul's oldies and releasing them on Columbia's Hall of Fame label. As each remaining Capitol single reaches five years of age, it will be deleted and become eligible to appear on Columbia, a process that should be completed after 1983 (provided McCartney resigns with the label when his contract expires in 1982). Interesting to note is that McCartney's first two Columbia singles were already deleted and combined to make up the first of Paul's Hall of Fame offerings. Also, "Maybe I'm Amazed" was the original studio version from the McCARTNEY album, and thus appeared for the very first time in the United States as a single.

(JUST LIKE) STARTING OVER/WOMAN
JOHN LENNON

Geffen GGEF 0408

June 5, 1981

In keeping with Warner Brothers' policy of taking hit singles that have enjoyed extraordinary sales and combining the A-sides as back-to-back oldies, this Geffen reissue single featuring John's recent chart-toppers was released.

SILLY LOVE SONGS/
  Cook of the House

WINGS
Columbia 18-02171
June 12, 1981

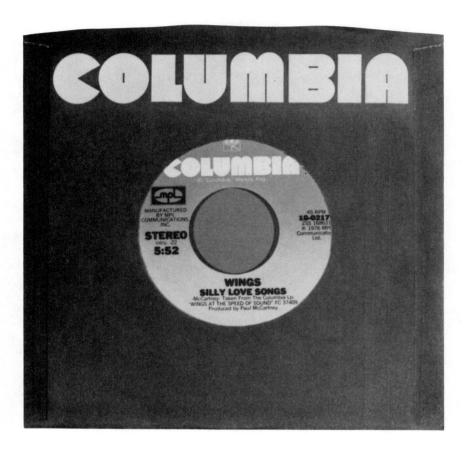

Another of the deleted Capitol singles that had expired according to the MPL lease, this was reissued by Columbia. However, unlike the previous four reissue McCartney singles, which had featured back-to-back A-sides and were placed on the Hall Of Fame oldies label, this disc retained its original B-side and appeared on the regular Columbia singles label.

ALL THOSE YEARS AGO/TEARDROPS
GEORGE HARRISON

Dark Horse GDRC 0410

WATCHING THE WHEELS/BEAUTIFUL BOY
JOHN LENNON

Geffen GGEF 0415

November 4, 1981

Warner Brothers issued the first back-to-back oldies single for Harrison (and the Dark Horse label) at the same time that they issued the second Lennon (Geffen) oldies single, which paired John's Top Ten hit "Watching the Wheels" with the track "Beautiful Boy" from DOUBLE FANTASY.

I WANT TO HOLD YOUR HAND/I Saw Her Standing There

Capitol Starline A-6278

CAN'T BUY ME LOVE/
   You Can't Do That

Capitol Starline A-6279

A HARD DAY'S NIGHT/
   I Should Have Known Better

Capitol Starline A-6281

I'LL CRY INSTEAD/I'm Happy Just to Dance with You

Capitol Starline A-6282

AND I LOVE HER/IF I FELL

Capitol Starline A-6283

MATCHBOX/SLOW DOWN

Capitol Starline A-6284

I FEEL FINE/
   She's a Woman

Capitol Starline A-6286

EIGHT DAYS A WEEK/I Don't Want to Spoil the Party

Capitol Starline A-6287

TICKET TO RIDE/
   Yes It Is

Capitol Starline A-6288

HELP!/
   I'm Down

Capitol Starline A-6290

YESTERDAY/
Act Naturally

Capitol Starline A-6291

WE CAN WORK IT OUT/DAY TRIPPER

Capitol Starline A-6293

NOWHERE MAN/
What Goes On

Capitol Starline A-6294

PAPERBACK WRITER/
Rain

Capitol Starline A-6296

YELLOW SUBMARINE/ ELEANOR RIGBY

Capitol Starline A-6297

PENNY LANE/ STRAWBERRY FIELDS FOREVER

Capitol Starline A-6299

ALL YOU NEED IS LOVE/
Baby You're a Rich Man

Capitol Starline A-6300

THE BEATLES
November 30, 1981 (August 31, 1981)

Capitol transferred seventeen of its twenty-eight Beatles singles to its Starline label, thus effectively deleting the actual Capitol label (and original catalog number) issues. Unlike previous Starline singles, all of these records retained their original B-sides. Delays at the plant pushed back the scheduled appearance of this set by almost three months.

ALBUMS

THE ORIGINAL GREATEST HITS
THE BEATLES

Greatest GRC-1001
1964

Twist and Shout/I Want to Hold Your Hand/All My Loving/Please Please Me/From Me to You/Do You Want to Know a Secret/Love Me Do/Can't Buy Me Love/Roll Over Beethoven/Please Mr. Postman/I'll Get You/She Loves You

This was the first Beatles bootleg album, which was so widely distributed throughout the United States that many people thought it was a legal issue. Though it never charted, it reportedly sold quite well. It is interesting to note that it contained the original 1962 (version one) single version of "Love Me Do," which would never officially be available in the United States until the 1980 release of RARITIES by Capitol.

THE SAVAGE YOUNG BEATLES
THE BEATLES featuring Tony Sheridan
(also: Tony Sheridan and the Beat Brothers)

Savage BM-69
1964

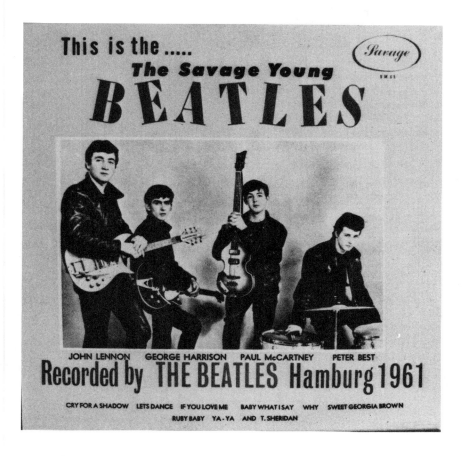

Cry for a Shadow/If You Love Me /
Sweet Georgia Brown/Why/(addi-
tional tracks by Tony Sheridan and the
Beat Brothers)

Four of the Beatles/Tony Sheridan 1961 Hamburg tracks appeared on this legally questionable album, which appeared magically in the record racks around America in the
middle of 1964. It would be reprinted several times again in the future, causing it to
pop up suddenly from time to time, only to disappear again.

THE GREAT AMERICAN TOUR—1965 LIVE BEATLEMANIA CONCERT
Ed Rudy "Tribute" (with the Liverpool Lads and THE BEATLES)

Lloyds E.R.M.C. Ltd. Records
1965

1965 Live BEATLEmania Concert/
1965 Live BEATLEmania Concert

This was the third and final Ed Rudy album dealing with the Beatles. Whereas the first two were actual interview records featuring the group, this effort was of an entirely different nature. Rudy may have called it a "tribute" album, but for all practical and legal purposes, this was the first live Beatles bootleg.

Rudy recorded one of the Beatles' American concerts during their second U.S. tour in 1964. That recording was placed on this record. On top of the Beatles, Rudy overdubbed the Liverpool Lads. The result was preposterous, with the real Beatles singing and playing in the background, and the Liverpool Lads singing and playing right over them in the foreground. In between numbers, you could actually hear the Beatles talking to the audience and introducing the songs. Spliced between the concert material were interviews with fans at the concert and in the studio.

This album did not receive very wide distribution and disappeared even faster than the second Rudy interview album had just before it.

THIS IS WHERE IT STARTED
THE BEATLES featuring Tony Sheridan
  (also: Tony Sheridan and the Beat Brothers, the Titans)

Metro MS-563
August 15, 1966

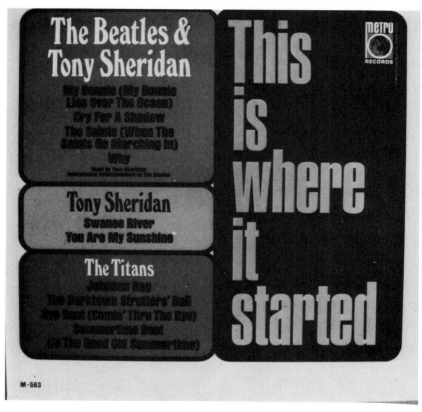

My Bonnie/Cry for a Shadow/The
Saints/Why/(additional tracks by Tony
Sheridan and the Beat Brothers; The
Titans)

One week after the release of REVOLVER, MGM reissued their 1964 album, THE
BEATLES WITH TONY SHERIDAN AND THEIR GUESTS, with a new title, THIS IS
WHERE IT STARTED, on a subsidiary label, Metro. Besides cover design, the only other
change was in the deletion of two songs by the Titans; otherwise, this was the same
record as before. Obviously most fans were well aware of this, and they wisely ignored
this reattempted ripoff.

THE AMAZING BEATLES (AND OTHER GREAT ENGLISH GROUP SOUNDS)
THE BEATLES featuring Tony Sheridan
(also: the Swallows)

Clarion 601
October 17, 1966

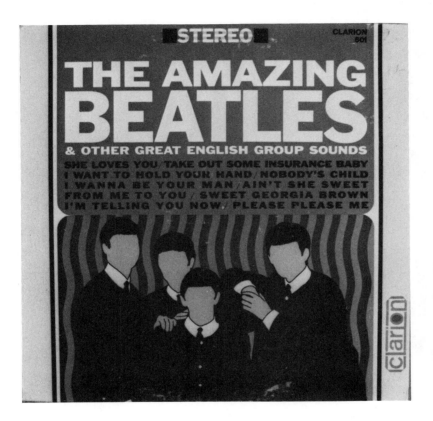

Ain't She Sweet/Take Out Some Insurance on Me, Baby/Nobody's Child/Sweet Georgia Brown/(additional tracks by the Swallows)

Two years and two weeks after Atco originally issued the AIN'T SHE SWEET album, a subsidiary label, Clarion, reissued the same recording. Changes in cover, title, and order of songs were made in a clear effort once more to induce unsuspecting Beatles fans into falling for the album.

Issued just two months after MGM/Metro had attempted the same thing, fortunately this record also failed to sell very well.

THE FAMILY WAY
George Martin and his Orchestra

London MS-82007
June 12, 1967

Love in the Open Air (cuts one through seven)/Love in the Open Air (cuts one through seven)

Paul McCartney wrote the entire soundtrack score for the motion picture *The Family Way,* and this record is noted here only because of the use of McCartney's name on the album cover. Since there were no solo Beatles bins back in 1967, this album was kept in the soundtrack section of the record store, where most of the copies stayed until returned to the factory, as it never sold well enough to chart.

ALPHA OMEGA (VOLUME ONE)
THE BEATLES

Audio Tape Inc. ATRBH-3583
Early 1973

Act Naturally/All I've Got to Do/All My Loving/And I Love Her/Baby's in Black/Yesterday/The Ballad of John and Yoko/Bangla Desh/Can't Buy Me Love/Come Together/Day Tripper/Do You Want to Know a Secret/Eight Days a Week/ Eleanor Rigby//Uncle Albert/ Admiral Halsey//I Should Have Known Better/It Won't Be Long/I Want to Hold Your Hand/Lady Madonna/Ticket to Ride/Lucy in the Sky with Diamonds/Michelle/Mr. Moonlight/I Feel Fine/If I Fell/I'll Be Back/Hey Jude/I'm a Loser/I'm Happy Just to Dance With You/I Saw Her Standing There/Nowhere Man/Ob-La-Di Ob-La-Da/Paperback Writer/Penny Lane/ Help!/Roll Over Beethoven/Sgt. Pepper's Lonely Hearts Club Band/Get Back/Hello Goodbye/Revolution 1/Here Comes the Sun/I'll Follow the Sun/Imagine/Honey Don't/We Can Work It Out/With a Little Help from My Friends/Yellow Submarine/Baby You're a Rich Man/You Can't Do That/ You've Got to Hide Your Love Away/Maybe I'm Amazed/A Hard Day's Night/She Loves You/Something/Strawberry Fields Forever/Tell Me Why/ The Long and Winding Road/Let It Be/Everybody's Trying to Be My Baby

This four-record boxed set was the unauthorized Beatles greatest hits collection that was hawked via TV ads in early 1973 in several parts of the United States, prompting Apple/Capitol/EMI into hurriedly packaging and releasing in April THE BEATLES 1962–1966 and THE BEATLES 1967–1970. In addition, Capitol saw to it that the TV ads for the Alpha Omega product were stopped, and the album subsequently disappeared from the market. (Interesting sidenote is that despite this course of action, Alpha Omega went on to release two additional volumes, another four-record boxed set, VOLUME TWO, and a two-record album, VOLUME THREE, in the following months.)

ROOTS (JOHN LENNON SINGS THE GREAT ROCK & ROLL HITS)
JOHN LENNON

Adam VIII A8018
February 1975

**Be-Bop-A-Lula/Ain't That a Shame/
Stand by Me/Sweet Little Sixteen/Rip
It Up/Angel Baby/Do You Want to
Dance/You Can't Catch Me/Bony
Moronie/Peggy Sue/Bring It on Home
to Me/Slippin' and Slidin'/Be My
Baby/Ya Ya/Just Because**

In early 1975, Adam VIII Records of New York began advertising a brand new John Lennon album available only via TV mail order—which turned out to be the rock 'n' roll oldies collection titled ROOTS.

Adam VIII owner Morris Levy claimed he had made a deal personally with Lennon, authorizing the release of ROOTS. When it finally got to court, Lennon admitted that he had given Levy a tape ("a rough mix") of the album, but that no deal had ever been finalized. Apple/Capitol got a court order barring Adam VIII from advertising or selling any more copies of ROOTS, and rush released the official ROCK 'N' ROLL album in mid-February.

Besides containing different mixes and longer fade-outs, ROOTS also featured two songs not released on the Apple album, "Angel Baby" and "Be My Baby."

SGT. PEPPER'S LONELY HEARTS CLUB BAND
THE BEATLES

Capitol SEAX-11840 (Limited Edition picture disc)
August 1978

(all tracks identical to original issue)

The record industry's picture disc craze of 1978 led to the release of the first of three Beatles-related picture disc albums from Capitol. To coincide with the opening of the *Sgt. Pepper* motion picture, starring Peter Frampton and the Bee Gees, Capitol issued this special picture disc version of the Beatles famed original. It was said that 150,000 copies made up the Limited Edition run.

THE BEATLES ("White Album")
THE BEATLES

Capitol SEBX-11841 (Limited Edition on white vinyl)

THE BEATLES 1962–1966
THE BEATLES

Capitol SEBX-11842 (Limited Edition on red vinyl)

THE BEATLES 1967–1970
THE BEATLES

Capitol SEBX-11843 (Limited Edition on blue vinyl)

August 1978

(all tracks identical to original issues)

Coinciding with the release of the SGT. PEPPER picture disc were these double-albums pressed on colored vinyl. These made for very special and attractive gift items, not to mention instant collector's editions. As with the picture disc, Capitol claimed a run of 150,000 Limited Edition copies for each.

ABBEY ROAD
THE BEATLES

Capitol SEAX-11900 (Limited Edition picture disc)

BAND ON THE RUN
PAUL McCARTNEY AND WINGS

Capitol SEAX-11901 (Limited Edition picture disc)

December 1978

(all tracks identical to original issues)

For the Christmas season, Capitol issued two additional Beatles-related picture discs. This time the nod went to the Beatles ABBEY ROAD, and to Paul McCartney and Wings' BAND ON THE RUN, two of the label's all-time biggest sellers. Capitol once more marked the Limited Edition set at 150,000 for each.

THE BEATLES COLLECTION
THE BEATLES

EMI/Capitol (Limited Edition deluxe boxed set)

Contained the following thirteen albums:
PLEASE PLEASE ME (UK release, Parlophone PCS-3042)
WITH THE BEATLES (UK release, Parlophone PCS-3045)
A HARD DAY'S NIGHT (UK release, Parlophone PCS-3058)
BEATLES FOR SALE (UK release, Parlophone PCS-3062)
HELP! (UK release, Parlophone PCS-3071)
RUBBER SOUL (UK release, Parlophone PCS-3075)
REVOLVER (UK release, Parlophone PCS-7009)
SGT. PEPPER'S LONELY HEARTS CLUB BAND (UK release,
  Parlophone PCS-7027)
THE BEATLES ("White Album") (UK release, Apple PCS-7067,
  7068)
YELLOW SUBMARINE (UK release, Apple PCS-7070)
ABBEY ROAD (UK release, Apple PCS-7088)
LET IT BE (UK release, Apple PCS-7096)
included was a special bonus promotional album:
RARITIES

Capitol SPRO-8969

December 1978

Another of Capitol's Beatles Christmas treats for 1978 was this extremely limited Limited Edition deluxe boxed set containing twelve of the group's original British releases, plus a thirteenth bonus album, which was a brand new compilation of assorted B-sides and other "lost" tracks, titled RARITIES. This was the only actual American Capitol Records album in the set (the other twelve were UK Parlophone albums).

Even with a list price of $132.98, Capitol had no trouble at all in quickly selling all 3,000 numbered copies to the public. Reportedly, there were 3,050 boxed sets in all, with the first fifty sets going to Capitol executives and assorted record industry brass as Christmas gifts. Thus, with such a small pressing, most fans had to settle for imported boxed sets from England, Holland, Japan, and Australia once the American sets were long gone.

The biggest let-down for boxed-set owners came a few short months later, when EMI released the RARITIES album on its own, in direct opposition to a statement issued with the release of THE BEATLES COLLECTION that had said that the *only* way anyone could obtain RARITIES would be to buy the boxed set. Many sets were sold on this basis alone. A few months later, RARITIES was available by itself on import for about $7.

RARITIES
THE BEATLES

Capitol SPRO-8969
December 1978

RARITIES
THE BEATLES

Capitol SN-12009
November 1979 (unreleased)

RARITIES
THE BEATLES

Capitol SHAL-12060
March 24, 1980

Across the Universe/Yes It Is/This Boy/The Inner Light/I'll Get You/Thank You Girl/I Want to Hold Your Hand/You Know My Name (Look Up My Number)/She Loves You/Rain/She's a Woman/Matchbox/I Call Your Name/Bad Boy/Slow Down/I'm Down/Long Tall Sally

(contents identical to **SPRO-8969**)

**Love Me Do/Misery/There's a Place/
Sie Liebt Dich/And I Love Her/Help!/
I'm Only Sleeping/I Am the Walrus/
Penny Lane/Helter Skelter/Don't Pass
Me By/The Inner Light/Across the
Universe/You Know My Name (Look Up
My Number)/Sgt. Pepper Inner Groove**

When EMI in England first packaged THE BEATLES COLLECTION boxed set in 1978, they included a brand new Beatles album made up of assorted B-sides, EP leftovers, and other assorted tracks that had never been included on any UK Beatles album.

For Capitol's Limited Edition release of THE BEATLES COLLECTION boxed set in America, an American version of RARITIES was prepared. The line-up was identical to the UK version, except that the obscure German-sung "Sie Liebt Dich" and "Komm Gib Mir Diene Hand" were substituted with the much rarer English-sung "She Loves You" and "I Want to Hold Your Hand." To top it off, this "extra" album, announced as being available *only* in the boxed set, and *not* to be released separately, was issued by Capitol in a *paper* sleeve (*every* other country releasing THE BEATLES COLLECTION— England, Australia, Holland, Japan and Brazil—issued RARITIES in a normal cardboard album jacket).

In the fall of 1979, EMI decided it would be a good idea after all to release RARITIES as a separate album on its own, and did so soon thereafter in a number of countries. In the United States, Capitol announced that RARITIES would be released as a budget line album (SN-12009), with content identical to that of their boxed set promotional version (SPRO-8969), and would be placed in the same plain blue jacket as the EMI issue.

However, as Capitol was preparing to release their budget line version, a very interesting alleged Capitol promotional album titled COLLECTORS ITEMS (SPRO-9462) appeared during the summer. It contained a line-up of rarities that seemed more suitable to American needs (the EMI compilation had been designed solely for UK fans).

By October, Capitol had begun pressing copies of their budget-line RARITIES (SN-12009) when they apparently discovered COLLECTORS ITEMS. Noting the decidedly superior song line-up and overall production values (including a full-color cover sporting a ton of rare Beatles memorabilia) of the unauthorized collection, Capitol quickly realized they had better reevaluate their RARITIES plans. They did, and it was soon announced that the budget album would be scrapped. In its place, Capitol would release a revised RARITIES album more tailored for U.S. buyers.

In March 1980, Capitol's revised RARITIES (SHAL-12060) was finally released. It sold quite well, due not only to the improved track selection but also to the fact that Capitol packaged the album more commercially with many photos of the group, including the original uncropped version of the infamous "Butcher" photo from 1966.

FIRST LIVE RECORDINGS—VOLUME ONE
Pickwick SPC-3361

FIRST LIVE RECORDINGS—VOLUME TWO
Pickwick SPC-3362

Where Have You Been All My Life/A Taste of Honey/Your Feet's Too Big/Mr. Moonlight/Besame Mucho/I'm Gonna Sit Right Down and Cry Over You/Be-Bop-A-Lula/Hallelujah I Love Her So/Till There Was You/Sweet Little Sixteen/Little Queenie//Kansas City/Hey Hey Hey Hey//Hully Gully

Ain't Nothin' Shakin'/Everybody's Trying to Be My Baby/Matchbox/ Talkin' 'Bout You/Long Tall Sally/Roll Over Beethoven/Hippy Hippy Shake/ Falling in Love Again/Lend Me Your Comb/Sheila/Red Sails in the Sunset/ To Know Her Is to Love Her/Shimmy Shake/I Remember You

THE BEATLES
January 24, 1979

A year and a half after its initial U.S. release, Pickwick Records obtained the rights to reissue the Atlantic/Lingasong collection of the Beatles live in Hamburg, 1962, recordings. Pickwick rearranged the order of the tracks, and issued them as two separate single albums with corresponding artwork, and designated them Volume One and Volume Two.

An almost unnoticed bonus was the inclusion of a song, "Hully Gully," that had not appeared on any other version of the Hamburg album worldwide, nor had it ever been listed in any of the previously published lists denoting the contents of the original 1962 tape. Many suspected the track was, in fact, by another of the groups that also appeared on the tape, and that its appearance here was an unintentional error.

Both volumes received wide distribution, and their budget line price tag no doubt enabled many more persons finally to experience the raw live performance of the early Beatles.

LET IT BE
THE BEATLES

Capitol SW-11922
March 1979

A HARD DAY'S NIGHT
THE BEATLES

Capitol SW-11921
August 1980

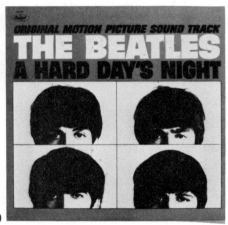

(all tracks identical to original issues)

In early 1979, it was announced that Capitol Records was going to reissue LET IT BE and A HARD DAY'S NIGHT, which up until that time had both been distributed in the United States by United Artists.

LET IT BE had actually been out of print in the States for a number of years, but was finally made available once again by Capitol, with the only notable change being that the reissue did not feature a fold-open cover as had the original.

Legal entanglements between United Artists and Capitol kept A HARD DAY'S NIGHT, originally set for release the same day as LET IT BE, from appearing on the Capitol label until the summer of 1980.

COLLECTORS ITEMS
THE BEATLES

Capitol SPRO-9462 (first edition)
Capitol SPRO-9463 (second edition)
August 4, 1979

9462 edition Love Me Do/Thank You Girl/From Me to You/All My Loving/ This Boy/Sie Liebt Dich/I Feel Fine/ She's a Woman/Help!/I'm Down/ Penny Lane/Baby, You're a Rich Man/ I Am the Walrus/The Inner Light/ Across the Universe/You Know My Name (Look Up My Number)/(Sgt. Pepper Inner Groove) 9463 edition (same as above except "Paperback Writer" replaced "I'm Down")

This wonderfully unique album first appeared at the 1979 Chicago Beatlefest. It was the album that caused Capitol to scrap their budget RARITIES release scheduled for fall and totally revise the package that eventually was released in the spring of 1980. If one compares the contents and line-up of the two albums, it is not hard to see where Capitol came up with most of its selections.

COLLECTORS ITEMS was so widely assumed to be an actual promotional version of the then up-coming RARITIES album that Capitol reportedly received calls from radio stations around the country wanting to know where *their* copy of the album was. Despite all of the commotion it caused, the actual number of copies sold was said to be very low.

HEAR THE BEATLES TELL ALL
Interviews with THE BEATLES

Vee Jay PRO-202
December 12, 1979

**Jim Steck interviews John Lennon/
Dave Hull interviews John, Paul,
George, Ringo**

This album originally appeared in the early fall of 1964, when Vee Jay reportedly issued 7,000 copies as a promotion-only release to radio stations. One side contained a Jim Steck interview with John Lennon, while the other side featured Dave Hull interviewing all four Beatles. Lou Adler added background music and percussion to the disc.

The album was counterfeited from time to time over the years, most notably in 1976. Then, in late 1979, Vee Jay uncovered the original artwork, plates, and master tapes for the album, and, in conjunction with a request from a major national retail chain interested in doing an independent storewide Beatles-record promotion, decided to issue the album commercially to the general public for the very first time (more than fifteen years after the original promotional edition had appeared).

Despite having to negotiate its own independent national distribution deals, Vee Jay has reportedly enjoyed very considerable success with the one Beatles album release of theirs over which Capitol does not own control.

ABBEY ROAD
THE BEATLES

Mobile Fidelity/Capitol MSFL 1-023
  (Original Half-Speed Master Recording)
December 28, 1979 (January 14, 1980)

(all tracks identical to original issue)

In late December 1979, Mobile Fidelity Sound Labs released another special album in their "Original Half-Speed Master Recording" series. This release, which arrived in the stores just after Christmas, turned out to be the Beatles ABBEY ROAD.

The super high fidelity was achieved by total quality control, beginning with the use of the original master tape (actually, Capitol's own sub-master). The exclusive half-speed mastering technique insured the natural musical clarity and impact, and the high definition super-vinyl disc was custom pressed in Japan. It was further protected by a static-free inner sleeve and placed in a heavy duty protective cardboard package before being inserted into the thicker than normal album jacket. This utmost care and quality not only made for the ultimate ABBEY ROAD experience, but also for the most expensive, as this album sold in the neighborhood of $16–$18. The limited edition pressing was not to exceed 200,000 copies.

THE HISTORIC FIRST LIVE RECORDINGS
THE BEATLES

Pickwick PTP-2098
May 16, 1980

Where Have You Been All My Life/A Taste of Honey/Your Feet's Too Big/ Mr. Moonlight/Besame Mucho/I'm Gonna Sit Right Down and Cry Over You/Be-Bop-A-Lula/Ain't Nothin' Shakin' but the Leaves/Everybody's Trying to Be My Baby/Matchbox/I'm Talking About You/Long Tall Sally/Roll Over Beethoven/Hippy Hippy Shake/Hallelujah I Love Her So/Till There Was You/Sweet Little Sixteen/ Little Queenie//Kansas City/Hey Hey Hey Hey//Hully Gully/Falling in Love Again/Lend Me Your Comb/Sheila/Red Sails in the Sunset/To Know Her Is to Love Her/Shimmy Shake/I Remember You

Almost a year and a half after issuing this collection as two separate albums, Pickwick reissued the Beatles live in Hamburg, 1962, material once again, this time in a double-album package, complete with new artwork and liner notes.

As most stores still continued to carry the two single volumes (Pickwick kept them in print) it looked as though it might take some time before everyone even realized that Pickwick had put together a new double-package budget version of these overlooked but important first historic live recordings of the Beatles.

268

McCARTNEY
PAUL McCARTNEY

Columbia FC-36478

RAM
PAUL AND LINDA McCARTNEY

Columbia FC-36479

WILD LIFE
WINGS

Columbia FC-36480

RED ROSE SPEEDWAY
PAUL McCARTNEY AND WINGS

Columbia FC-36481

BAND ON THE RUN
PAUL McCARTNEY AND WINGS

Columbia FC-36482

May 22, 1980

VENUS AND MARS
WINGS

Columbia FC-36801

September 25, 1980

(all tracks identical to original issues)

When McCartney made the move from Capitol to Columbia in 1979, he also took the masters for all of his Capitol albums and singles, which he had leased to Capitol on a five-year basis. Under the leasing agreement, after five years from the original release date, ownership reverted to McCartney.

So, reissued simultaneously with the new McCARTNEY II album in May 1980 were McCartney and Wings' first five Capitol/Apple albums. Shortly thereafter, a sixth album (VENUS AND MARS) expired on Capitol and was subsequently reissued on Columbia.

Under this agreement, Paul's final Capitol product, WINGS GREATEST (released in late 1978), will be eligible for Columbia by the end of 1983 (provided that McCartney and Columbia opt to renew his original contract which is due to expire in 1982). In the meantime, all other McCartney product reaching five years of age will be available for reissue by Columbia.

ROCK 'N' ROLL MUSIC—VOLUME ONE
THE BEATLES

Capitol SN-16020

ROCK 'N' ROLL MUSIC—VOLUME TWO
THE BEATLES

Capitol SN-16021

(all tracks identical to original issue)

October 1980

Capitol reissued its first Beatles album product ever by deleting the 1976 ROCK 'N' ROLL MUSIC double album (SKBO-11537) and reissuing the contents as two separate single albums, complete with brand new covers, and designated VOLUME ONE and VOLUME TWO.

These albums had just been placed in the stores a few weeks prior to the death of John Lennon. Thus, in the rush for Beatles and Lennon product in the aftermath of the tragedy, they sold well enough actually to be charted, something a reissue album normally does not accomplish.

(Note: Because they did in fact make the charts, these two albums are covered in the normal album section of this book. Please see album section, October 1980.)

DARK HORSE
GEORGE HARRISON

Capitol SN-16055

MIND GAMES
JOHN LENNON

Capitol SN-16068

ROCK 'N' ROLL
JOHN LENNON

Capitol SN-16069

RINGO
RINGO STARR

Capitol SN-16114

(all tracks identical to original issues)

October 1980

Also tossed into the reissue budget-line series by Capitol were these four solo albums. Harrison's DARK HORSE featured an entirely new front and back cover design, while Ringo's hit album RINGO no longer featured a gatefold cover. The two Lennon albums remained exactly as before.

MAGICAL MYSTERY TOUR
THE BEATLES

Mobile Fidelity/Capitol MSFL 1-047
  (Original Half-Speed Master Recording)
January 30, 1981 (February 1, 1981)

(all tracks identical to original issue)

In early 1981, Mobile Fidelity Sound Labs released their second Beatles "Original Half-Speed Master Recording" album. Although this record was made with the usual care and precision craftsmanship of all those in Mobile Fidelity's series, it should be noted that the tape they received from Capitol Records, and from which the album was pressed, was not the original EMI master tape, but rather Capitol's own sub-master tape, which unfortunately presented three tracks ("Penny Lane," "All You Need Is Love," and "Baby You're a Rich Man") in reprocessed stereo, rather than true stereo, thus in effect somewhat defeating the whole purpose of the album.

LIVING IN THE MATERIAL WORLD
GEORGE HARRISON

Capitol SN-16216

EXTRA TEXTURE (READ ALL ABOUT IT)
GEORGE HARRISON

Capitol SN-16217

SENTIMENTAL JOURNEY
RINGO STARR

Capitol SN-16218

GOODNIGHT VIENNA
RINGO STARR

Capitol SN-16219

(all tracks identical to original issues)

February 1981

Two additional George Harrison and two additional Ringo Starr albums were placed on Capitol's budget line in early 1981. Only the Harrison albums differed significantly from the original Apple releases. LIVING IN THE MATERIAL WORLD no longer featured a gatefold cover, and also had song titles and musician credits added to the back cover. EXTRA TEXTURE suffered the loss of its textured and die-cut cover as well as the double-photo inner sleeve.

This brought to ten the number of Capitol Beatles and ex-Beatles albums to be placed on the reissue budget line.

TIMELESS
Interviews with THE BEATLES

**Silhouette Music SM-10004 (Limited Edition picture disc)
March 1, 1981**

Limited Edition
Picture Disc

SILHOUETTE
MUSIC
S.M.-10004

PREVIOUSLY UNRELEASED INTERVIEWS WITH THE BEATLES

(Press conference excerpts) Vancouver, Canada 1964/Chicago, 1966/ newscast about John Lennon/(additional tracks featuring cover versions and tributes by various musicians)

A few months after the death of John Lennon, this album appeared on the market, initially as a mail-order item, and soon thereafter as a regular store item.

Of the album's nine cuts, only two feature the Beatles, in excerpts from their press conferences in Vancouver 1964 and Chicago 1966. Of the remaining seven, one is a newscast about John Lennon, and the other six include Lennon, Beatles, and Beatles-tribute songs performed by some studio musicians.

This limited edition release was originally planned for 10,000 copies, but due to buyer demand was upped to a total of 25,000.

DAWN OF THE SILVER BEATLES
THE (SILVER) BEATLES

PAC Records UDL 2333 (Limited Edition)
April 16, 1981 (April 2, 1981)

Love of the Loved/Money/Sure to Fall/
Take Good Care of My Baby/Three
Cool Cats/Like Dreamers Do/Crying,
Waiting, Hoping/Searchin'/Till There
Was You/Memphis

Another release of dubious legal status to follow Lennon's death was this offering from PAC Records, which featured ten tracks from the Beatles alleged "Decca Audition Tape" circa January 1962, and featuring Pete Best on drums. Initially, this album was made available to the public only through mail orders but was subsequently issued in record stores a few months after release.

This album had a Limited Edition run of 153,000, and was reportedly numbered in two ways. The first 750 copies issued were hand stamped with the serial numbers 00251–001000, while the remainder of the albums were numbered by the use of a registration card (numbers 001999–153,000).

As for the material itself, these high-quality recordings showcased the early Beatles' talent not only for covering and adapting hits of the day but for writing their own original compositions as well—none of which have ever been officially released (at least until this record came along). These recordings provided another valuable insight into the historic shaping and fine-tuning of the group that went on to take the world by storm.

LIGHTNING STRIKES TWICE
Elvis Presley/THE (SILVER) BEATLES

PAC Records UDL 2382
1981

Sheik of Araby/To Know Him Is to Love Him/Hello Little Girl/September in the Rain/Besame Mucho (The Silver Beatles)/(additional tracks featuring Elvis Presley)

The questionable legality regarding DAWN OF THE SILVER BEATLES was nothing when compared to the ramifications of issuing a "legitimate" album composed of tracks featuring Elvis Presley on one side and the Beatles on the other.

The Beatles material included here is the five remaining songs that made up the whole of the "Decca Audition Tape" and that were not on the DAWN OF THE SILVER BEATLES album. As for the Elvis material on this album, PAC Records claims the five recordings to be from 1952, although most Presley experts recognize the songs as being from the King's legendary Sun Records sessions a few years later (and which at last check, as with the rights of all Presley's Sun recordings, belong solely to RCA Records).

To further add to the oddness of this compilation, the album was issued in a blank white cover with small black printing and nothing more. Likewise with the label. There was no artwork whatsoever, even though the album carried a list price ($12.95) that was three dollars higher than that of DAWN OF THE SILVER BEATLES. Unlike that album though, this album was available only through mail order. However, by the end of the year, PAC Records had vanished from their Phoenix, Arizona, offices, leaving no forwarding address or other means of contact. Anybody releasing an album like this (as well as their other offerings) was bound to disappear at some point.

BAND ON THE RUN
PAUL McCARTNEY AND WINGS

Columbia HC 46482 (Half-Speed Master Audiophile Recording)
April 24, 1981

WINGS AT THE SPEED OF SOUND
WINGS

Columbia FC 37409
July 13, 1981

(all tracks identical to original issues)

In the spring of 1981, Columbia issued a special half-speed master recording of BAND ON THE RUN as part of their expanding audiophile series.

During the summer, Columbia reissued WINGS AT THE SPEED OF SOUND, which had recently been deleted by Capitol.

BEAUCOUPS OF BLUES
RINGO STARR

Capitol SN-16235

BLAST FROM YOUR PAST
RINGO STARR

Capitol SN-16236

(all tracks identical to original issues)

September 1981

With these two reissues, Capitol's entire catalog of five Ringo Starr albums was now available on the label's budget line reissue series. The only notable difference this time around was BEAUCOUPS OF BLUES, which no longer featured a gatefold cover.

278

IN THE BEGINNING
THE BEATLES
(also: THE BEATLES featuring Tony Sheridan; Tony Sheridan and the Beat Brothers)

Polydor 24-4504
October 1981

(all tracks identical to original issue)

This reissue appeared eleven and a half years after the initial Polydor release. It was identical to the original save for the single jacket that had replaced the gatefold sleeve, thus eliminating some nice early photographs of the Beatles in Hamburg.

THE AMERICAN TOUR WITH ED RUDY
Ed Rudy interviews THE BEATLES

INS Radio News Documentary 2
1981

(Contents same as original)

Several months after the death of John Lennon, this album was reissued. According to the mail order ads which appeared around the country, Mr. Rudy would personally autograph the album if desired—an offer no other "fifth" Beatle has ever matched!

LIVE AT THE STAR CLUB, 1962, HAMBURG, GERMANY
THE BEATLES

Hall of Music HMI 2200
1981

Roll Over Beethoven/Hippy Hippy Shake/Sweet Little Sixteen/Taste of Honey/Till There Was You/I Saw Her Standing There/Ask Me Why/Reminiscing/Twist and Shout/Kansas City/Mr. Moonlight/Long Tall Sally/Little Queenie/Be-Bop-A-Lula/Red Sails in the Sunset/Everybody's Trying to Be My Baby/Matchbox/Talkin' Bout You

Hall of Music became the third American record label to release this set of historic live early Beatles recordings. However, it is already becoming apparent that these songs, recorded in Hamburg, Germany in 1962 are destined for the same recycle treatment that the group's 1961 Hamburg recordings (with Tony Sheridan) have undergone, and thus, will most likely be made available every couple of years via a variety of labels, covers and packages.

THE BEATLES ("White Album")
THE BEATLES

Mobile Fidelity/Capitol MFSL 2-072
  (Original Half-Speed Master Recording)
January 7, 1982

(all tracks identical to original issue)

For the third year in a row, Mobile Fidelity began its new year by releasing another special Beatles half-speed master recording album, this time choosing the group's famous "White Album."

FIRST MOVEMENT
THE BEATLES featuring Tony Sheridan

Phoenix PHX 339
April 1982

Cry for a Shadow/Let's Dance/If You
Love Me Baby/What'd I Say/Sweet
Georgia Brown/Ruby Baby/Ya Ya/Why

Only six months after this same material was recycled via the reissue of Polydor's IN THE BEGINNING album, Phoenix Records released this repackage of the Beatles 1961 Hamburg sessions with Tony Sheridan. In spite of the fact that these recordings have been reissued more than half a dozen times in the United States (on as many different labels!) this album carried a sticker on the front proclaiming: "Attention collectors—unreleased tracks." After nearly twenty years, the hype and promotion of these recordings has not changed a bit.

ALBUMS BY VARIOUS ARTISTS FEATURING BEATLES TRACKS

CHARTBUSTERS VOLUME FOUR

Capitol ST-2094
May 11, 1964

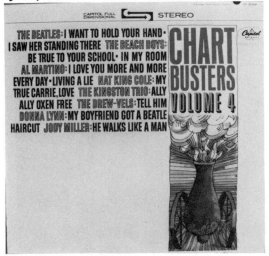

"I Want to Hold Your Hand"
"I Saw Her Standing There"

THE BIG HITS FROM ENGLAND AND THE USA

Capitol DT-2125
September 7, 1964

"Can't Buy Me Love"
"You Can't Do That"

DISCOTHEQUE IN ASTROSOUND

(BEATLES featuring Tony Sheridan)
Clarion 609
November 28, 1966
"Take Out Some Insurance Baby"

FIRST VIBRATION

Do It Now Foundation 5000
May 1969
"Nowhere Man"

DO IT NOW

Do It Now Foundation LP 1001
February 1971
"Nowhere Man"

FLASHBACK GREATS OF THE 60's

(BEATLES featuring Tony Sheridan)
K-Tel TU-229
October 1973
"My Bonnie"

HISTORY OF BRITISH ROCK — VOLUME TWO

Sire SASH-3705
December 2, 1974
"Ain't She Sweet"

HISTORY OF BRITISH ROCK — VOLUME THREE

(BEATLES featuring Tony Sheridan)
Sire SASH-3712
October 27, 1975
"My Bonnie"

BRITISH GOLD

Sire R-224095
1978
"Ain't She Sweet"

BRITISH ROCK CLASSICS

(BEATLES featuring Tony Sheridan)
Sire R-234021
1979
"My Bonnie"

Various Artists' Albums Featuring Individual Beatles Tracks

TOMMY

London Symphony Orchestra
RINGO STARR as Uncle Ernie
Ode SP-99001
November 27, 1972
"Fiddle About"
"Tommy's Holiday Camp"

The albums LIVE AND LET DIE (Original Soundtrack) and CONCERTS FOR THE PEOPLE OF KAMPUCHEA featuring tracks by PAUL McCARTNEY AND WINGS are covered in the regular album release section.

APPENDIX II

United States Quick Reference Chart Supplements and Totals

SINGLES
   (B-sides listed in parentheses)
THE BEATLES
JOHN LENNON
PAUL McCARTNEY
GEORGE HARRISON
RINGO STARR

ALBUMS
THE BEATLES
JOHN LENNON
PAUL McCARTNEY
GEORGE HARRISON
RINGO STARR

NUMBER ONE SINGLES
NUMBER ONE ALBUMS

THE BEATLES

SINGLES	BB	CB	RW	'BEST'
PLEASE PLEASE ME	—	—	—	—
FROM ME TO YOU	116	—	—	116
SHE LOVES YOU	1	1	1	1
ROLL OVER BEETHOVEN	68	30	35	30
I WANT TO HOLD YOUR HAND/	1	1	1	1
(I SAW HER STANDING THERE)	(14)	—	—	(14)
MY BONNIE	26	29	31	26
PLEASE PLEASE ME/	3	3	3	3
(FROM ME TO YOU)	(41)	—	(46)	(41)
ALL MY LOVING	45	31	32	31
TWIST AND SHOUT/	2	1	1	1
(THERE'S A PLACE)	(74)	—	—	(74)
CAN'T BUY ME LOVE/	1	1	1	1
(YOU CAN'T DO THAT)	(48)	—	—	(48)
THE BEATLES (EP)	—	—	—	—
DO YOU WANT TO KNOW A SECRET/	2	3	3	2

SINGLES	BB	CB	RW	'BEST'
(THANK YOU GIRL)	(35)	—	(39)	(35)
WHY	88	—	—	88
LOVE ME DO/	1	1	1	1
(P.S. I LOVE YOU)	(10)	(10)	(13)	(10)
FOUR BY THE BEATLES (EP)	92	86	—	86
SIE LIEBT DICH	97	—	—	97
SWEET GEORGIA BROWN	—	—	—	—
AIN'T SHE SWEET	19	14	13	13
A HARD DAY'S NIGHT/	1	1	1	1
(I SHOULD HAVE KNOWN BETTER)	(53)	—	—	(53)
I'LL CRY INSTEAD/	25	22	28	22
(I'M HAPPY JUST TO DANCE WITH YOU)	(95)	—	—	(95)
AND I LOVE HER/	12	—	16	12
IF I FELL	(53)	14	(59)	14
MATCHBOX/	17	17	22	17
(SLOW DOWN)	(25)	(34)	(23)	(23)
I FEEL FINE/	1	1	1	1
(SHE'S A WOMAN)	(4)	(8)	(8)	(4)
4 BY THE BEATLES (EP)	68	68	—	68
EIGHT DAYS A WEEK/	1	1	1	1
(I DON'T WANT TO SPOIL THE PARTY)	(39)	—	—	(39)
TICKET TO RIDE/	1	1	1	1
(YES IT IS)	(46)	—	—	(46)
HELP!/	1	1	1	1
(I'M DOWN)	(101)	—	—	(101)
YESTERDAY/	1	1	1	1
(ACT NATURALLY)	(47)	(28)	—	(28)
BOYS/	102	73	—	73
(KANSAS CITY)	—	75	—	(75)
WE CAN WORK IT OUT/	1	1	1	1
(DAY TRIPPER)	(5)	(10)	(15)	(5)
NOWHERE MAN/	3	2	1	1
(WHAT GOES ON)	(81)	—	—	(81)
PAPERBACK WRITER/	1	1	1	1
(RAIN)	(23)	(31)	—	(23)
YELLOW SUBMARINE/	2	1	1	1
(ELEANOR RIGBY)	(11)	(12)	(16)	(11)
PENNY LANE/	1	1	1	1
(STRAWBERRY FIELDS FOREVER)	(8)	(11)	(9)	(8)
ALL YOU NEED IS LOVE/	1	1	1	1
(BABY YOU'RE A RICH MAN)	(34)	(65)	(60)	(34)
HELLO GOODBYE/	1	1	1	1

SINGLES	BB	CB	RW	'BEST'
(I AM THE WALRUS)	(56)	(46)	—	(46)
LADY MADONNA/	4	2	2	2
(THE INNER LIGHT)	(96)	—	—	(96)
HEY JUDE/	1	1	1	1
(REVOLUTION)	(12)	—	(2)	(2)
GET BACK/	1	1	1	1
(DON'T LET ME DOWN)	(35)	—	—	(35)
BALLAD OF JOHN AND YOKO	8	10	7	7
SOMETHING/	3	2	—	2
COME TOGETHER	2	1	—	1
SOMETHING/COME TOGETHER	1	—	1	1
LET IT BE	1	1	1	1
LONG AND WINDING ROAD/FOR YOU BLUE	1	1	1	1
GOT TO GET YOU INTO MY LIFE	7	3	9	3
OB-LA-DI OB-LA-DA	49	47	75	47
SGT. PEPPER'S LONELY HEARTS CLUB BAND/ WITH A LITTLE HELP FROM MY FRIENDS	71	92	103	71
THE BEATLES MOVIE MEDLEY	12	14	(39)	12

TOTALS	BB	CB	RW	'BEST'
TOTAL singles released: 47*				
TOTAL singles charted	44	42	37	44
TOTAL entries charted	70	53	49	71
NUMBER ONE singles	20	22	23	23
TOP TEN singles	28	28	28	29
TOP TEN entries	32	31	31	34
TOP TWENTY singles	32	32	30	33
TOP TWENTY entries	40	36	34	42
TOP THIRTY singles	34	35	32	39
TOP THIRTY entries	44	40	35	48
TOP FORTY singles	34	36	36	40
TOP FORTY entries	48	43	37	53
TOP 100 singles	42	41	37	43
TOP 100 entries	67	53	37	69

*47 total includes 42 U.S. singles, including one Capitol Starline reissue, 2 Capitol of Canada import singles, and 3 EP's.

Not included in above totals:

MY BONNIE	—	—	—	—

(1962 Decca release: Tony Sheridan and the Beat Brothers)

JOHN LENNON (w/PLASTIC ONO BAND; YOKO ONO)

SINGLES	BB	CB	RW	'BEST'
GIVE PEACE A CHANCE	14	11	10	10
COLD TURKEY	30	32	26	26
INSTANT KARMA	3	3	3	3
MOTHER	43	19	16	16
POWER TO THE PEOPLE	11	10	8	8
IMAGINE	3	2	1	1
HAPPY XMAS (WAR IS OVER)	—	36	28	28
WOMAN IS THE NIGGER OF THE WORLD	57	—	87	57
MIND GAMES	18	10	10	10
WHATEVER GETS YOU THRU THE NIGHT	1	1	1	1
#9 DREAM	9	10	17	9
STAND BY ME	20	20	24	20
(JUST LIKE) STARTING OVER	1	1	1	1
WOMAN	2	1	2	1
WATCHING THE WHEELS	10	7	9	7

TOTALS	BB	CB	RW	'BEST'
TOTAL singles released: 15				
TOTAL singles charted	14	14	15	15
NUMBER ONE singles	2	3	3	4
TOP TEN singles	7	9	9	10
TOP TWENTY singles	11	12	11	12
TOP THIRTY singles	12	12	14	14
TOP FORTY singles	12	14	14	14
TOP 100 singles	14	14	15	15
Not included in above totals:				
GOD SAVE US/DO THE OZ (Elastic Oz Band)	—	—	112	112

PAUL McCARTNEY (w/WINGS; LINDA McCARTNEY)

SINGLES	BB	CB	RW	'BEST'
ANOTHER DAY/OH WOMAN OH WHY	5	6	5	5
UNCLE ALBERT/ADMIRAL HALSEY	1	1	1	1
GIVE IRELAND BACK TO THE IRISH	21	38	36	21

SINGLES	BB	CB	RW	'BEST'
MARY HAD A LITTLE LAMB	28	48	38	28
HI, HI, HI	10	6	7	6
MY LOVE	1	1	1	1
LIVE AND LET DIE	2	1	1	1
HELEN WHEELS	10	5	4	4
JET	7	5	5	5
BAND ON THE RUN	1	1	1	1
JUNIOR'S FARM/SALLY G	3	4	5	3
LISTEN TO WHAT THE MAN SAID	1	1	1	1
LETTING GO	39	41	62	39
VENUS AND MARS/ROCK SHOW	12	16	28	12
SILLY LOVE SONGS	1	1	1	1
LET 'EM IN	3	1	4	1
MAYBE I'M AMAZED	10	10	26	10
GIRL'S SCHOOL/MULL OF KINTYRE	33	31	33	31
WITH A LITTLE LUCK	1	1	1	1
I'VE HAD ENOUGH	25	28	30	25
LONDON TOWN	39	42	48	39
GOODNIGHT TONIGHT	5	4	7	4
GETTING CLOSER	20	20	22	20
ARROW THROUGH ME	28	36	27	27
WONDERFUL CHRISTMASTIME	—	—	—	—
COMING UP	1	2	3	1
WATERFALLS	106	—	83	83
EBONY AND IVORY	1	1	(40)	1

TOTALS	BB	CB	RW	'BEST'
TOTAL singles released: 28				
TOTAL singles charted	27	26	27	27
NUMBER ONE singles	8	9	7	10
TOP TEN singles	17	17	15	17
TOP TWENTY singles	19	19	15	19
TOP THIRTY singles	23	20	20	23
TOP FORTY singles	26	23	24	26
TOP 100 singles	26	26	27	27
Not included in above totals:				
WALKING IN THE PARK WITH ELOISE (Country Hams)	—	—	—	—
SEASIDE WOMAN (Suzy and the Red Stripes)	59	58	92	58

GEORGE HARRISON

SINGLES	BB	CB	RW	'BEST'
MY SWEET LORD/ISN'T IT A PITY	1	1	1	1
WHAT IS LIFE	10	7	10	7
BANGLA-DESH	23	20	13	13
GIVE ME LOVE	1	1	1	1
DARK HORSE	15	19	27	15
DING DONG* DING DONG	36	36	49	36
YOU	20	19	36	19
THIS GUITAR	—	—	—	—
THIS SONG	25	28	33	25
CRACKERBOX PALACE	19	17	26	17
BLOW AWAY	16	12	17	12
LOVE COMES TO EVERYONE	—	—	118	118
ALL THOSE YEARS AGO	2	3	3	2
TEARDROPS	102	88	—	88

TOTALS	BB	CB	RW	'BEST'
TOTAL singles released: 14				
TOTAL singles charted	12	12	12	13
NUMBER ONE singles	2	2	2	2
TOP TEN singles	4	4	4	4
TOP TWENTY singles	7	9	6	9
TOP THIRTY singles	10	10	8	10
TOP FORTY singles	11	11	10	11
TOP 100 singles	11	12	11	12

RINGO STARR

SINGLES	BB	CB	RW	'BEST'
BEAUCOUPS OF BLUES	87	69	87	69
IT DON'T COME EASY	4	1	1	1
BACK OFF BOOGALOO	9	10	8	8
PHOTOGRAPH	1	1	1	1
YOU'RE SIXTEEN	1	1	1	1
OH MY MY	5	6	5	5
ONLY YOU	5	6	9	5

SINGLES	BB	CB	RW	'BEST'
NO NO SONG/SNOOKEROO	3	1	3	1
GOODNIGHT VIENNA/OO WEE	31	29	54	29
A DOSE OF ROCK 'N' ROLL	26	26	32	26
HEY BABY	74	62	93	62
WINGS	—	—	119	119
DROWNING IN THE SEA OF LOVE	—	—	—	—
LIPSTICK TRACES	—	—	103	103
HEART ON MY SLEEVE	—	—	—	—
WRACK MY BRAIN	38	37	40	37
PRIVATE PROPERTY	—	—	—	—

TOTALS	BB	CB	RW	'BEST'
TOTAL singles released: 17				
Total singles charted	12	12	14	14
NUMBER ONE singles	2	4	3	4
TOP TEN singles	7	7	7	7
TOP TWENTY singles	7	7	7	7
TOP THIRTY singles	8	9	7	9
TOP FORTY singles	10	10	9	10
TOP 100 singles	12	12	12	12

THE BEATLES

ALBUMS	BB	CB	RW	'BEST'
INTRODUCING THE BEATLES	—	—	—	—
MEET THE BEATLES	1	1	1	1
INTRODUCING THE BEATLES	2	2	1	1
THE BEATLES WITH TONY SHERIDAN AND THEIR GUESTS	68	43	—	43
JOLLY WHAT! THE BEATLES AND FRANK IFIELD ON STAGE	104	73	—	73
THE BEATLES SECOND ALBUM	1	1	1	1
THE AMERICAN TOUR WITH ED RUDY	20	55	32	20
A HARD DAY'S NIGHT	1	1	1	1
SOMETHING NEW	2	2	2	2
THE BEATLES VS. THE FOUR SEASONS	142	—	—	142
AIN'T SHE SWEET	—	—	—	—

ALBUMS	BB	CB	RW	'BEST'
SONGS, PICTURES AND STORIES OF THE FABULOUS BEATLES	63	100	79	63
THE BEATLES STORY	7	7	13	7
BEATLES '65	1	1	1	1
ED RUDY WITH NEW U.S. TOUR	—	—	—	—
THE EARLY BEATLES	43	24	29	24
BEATLES VI	1	1	1	1
HELP!	1	1	1	1
RUBBER SOUL	1	1	1	1
YESTERDAY . . . AND TODAY	1	1	1	1
REVOLVER	1	1	1	1
SGT. PEPPER'S LONELY HEARTS CLUB BAND	1	1	1	1
MAGICAL MYSTERY TOUR	1	1	1	1
THE BEATLES ("White Album")	1	1	1	1
YELLOW SUBMARINE	2	3	2	2
ABBEY ROAD	1	1	1	1
HEY JUDE (THE BEATLES AGAIN)	2	2	1	1
IN THE BEGINNING	117	94	139	94
LET IT BE	1	1	1	1
THE BEATLES 1962–1966	3	1	4	1
THE BEATLES 1967–1970	1	2	1	1
ROCK 'N' ROLL MUSIC	2	4	2	2
THE BEATLES AT THE HOLLYWOOD BOWL	2	3	7	2
LIVE AT THE STAR CLUB IN HAMBURG, GERMANY, 1962	111	183	165	111
LOVE SONGS	24	28	36	24
THE BEATLES TAPES	—	—	—	—
BEATLE TALK	—	—	—	—
RARITIES	21	20	26	20
ROCK 'N' ROLL MUSIC — VOLUME ONE	—	—	134	134
ROCK 'N' ROLL MUSIC — VOLUME TWO	—	—	137	137
REEL MUSIC	19	18	(90)	18

TOTALS	BB	CB	RW	'BEST'
TOTAL albums released: 41*				
TOTAL albums charted	34	33	33	36
NUMBER ONE albums	15	15	17	18
TOP TEN albums	22	22	22	22
TOP TWENTY albums	24	24	23	25
TOP FIFTY albums	27	27	27	29

TOTALS	BB	CB	RW	'BEST'
TOP 100 albums	29	31	29	32
TOP 200 albums	34	33	33	36

*41 album total includes:
18 pre-split Capitol/Apple albums
 6 post-split Capitol/Apple compilation albums (not including one live album)
 2 post-split Capitol reissues that charted
 4 interview albums
 2 live albums
 3 Beatles featuring Tony Sheridan albums
 3 Vee Jay repackages of the complete INTRODUCING THE BEATLES album

JOHN LENNON (w/PLASTIC ONO BAND; YOKO ONO)

ALBUMS	BB	CB	RW	'BEST'
TWO VIRGINS	124	82	56	56
LIFE WITH THE LIONS	174	118	124	118
WEDDING ALBUM	178	—	108	108
LIVE PEACE IN TORONTO 1969	10	18	18	10
JOHN LENNON/PLASTIC ONO BAND	6	4	2	2
IMAGINE	1	1	1	1
SOMETIME IN NEW YORK CITY	48	26	30	26
MIND GAMES	9	6	7	6
WALLS AND BRIDGES	1	1	1	1
ROCK 'N' ROLL	6	6	4	4
SHAVED FISH	12	19	21	12
DOUBLE FANTASY	1	1	1	1

TOTALS	BB	CB	RW	'BEST'
TOTAL albums released: 12				
TOTAL albums charted	12	11	12	12
NUMBER ONE albums	3	3	3	3
TOP TEN albums	7	6	6	7
TOP TWENTY albums	8	8	8	8
TOP FIFTY albums	9	9	9	9
TOP 100 albums	9	10	10	10
TOP 200 albums	12	11	12	12

PAUL McCARTNEY (w/WINGS; LINDA McCARTNEY)

ALBUMS	BB	CB	RW	'BEST'
McCARTNEY	1	1	1	1
RAM	2	2	2	2
WILD LIFE	10	6	9	6
RED ROSE SPEEDWAY	1	1	1	1
BAND ON THE RUN	1	1	1	1
VENUS AND MARS	1	1	1	1
WINGS AT THE SPEED OF SOUND	1	1	1	1
WINGS OVER AMERICA	1	2	3	1
LONDON TOWN	2	2	2	2
WINGS GREATEST	29	21	23	21
BACK TO THE EGG	8	7	7	7
McCARTNEY II	3	3	3	3
THE McCARTNEY INTERVIEW	158	—	141	141
TUG OF WAR	1	1	*	1

TOTALS	BB	CB	RW	'BEST'
TOTAL albums released: 14				
TOTAL albums charted	14	13	13	14
NUMBER ONE albums	7	6	5	7
TOP TEN albums	12	12	11	12
TOP TWENTY albums	12	12	11	12
TOP FIFTY albums	13	13	12	13
TOP 100 albums	13	13	12	13
TOP 200 albums	14	13	13	14
Not included in above totals:				
LIVE AND LET DIE	17	20	17	17
(Soundtrack w/Wings)				
CONCERTS FOR THE PEOPLE OF KAMPUCHEA	36	31	31	31
(various w/Wings)				

GEORGE HARRISON

ALBUMS	BB	CB	RW	'BEST'
WONDERWALL MUSIC	49	39	33	33
ELECTRONIC SOUND	191	—	—	191
ALL THINGS MUST PASS	1	1	1	1

ALBUMS	BB	CB	RW	'BEST'
CONCERT FOR BANGLA DESH	2	2	1	1
LIVING IN THE MATERIAL WORLD	1	1	1	1
DARK HORSE	4	4	4	4
EXTRA TEXTURE (READ ALL ABOUT IT)	8	9	9	8
THE BEST OF GEORGE HARRISON	31	29	33	29
THIRTY THREE & ⅓	11	15	14	11
GEORGE HARRISON	14	12	17	12
SOMEWHERE IN ENGLAND	11	11	11	11

TOTALS	BB	CB	RW	'BEST'
TOTAL albums released: 11				
TOTAL albums charted	11	10	10	11
NUMBER ONE albums	2	2	3	3
TOP TEN albums	5	5	5	5
TOP TWENTY albums	8	8	8	8
TOP FIFTY albums	10	10	10	10
TOP 100 albums	10	10	10	10
TOP 200 albums	11	10	10	11

RINGO STARR

ALBUMS	BB	CB	RW	'BEST'
SENTIMENTAL JOURNEY	22	21	20	20
BEAUCOUPS OF BLUES	65	31	38	31
RINGO	2	1	1	1
GOODNIGHT VIENNA	8	8	5	5
BLAST FROM YOUR PAST	30	40	64	30
RINGO'S ROTOGRAVURE	28	56	45	28
RINGO THE 4th	162	194	178	162
BAD BOY	129	97	144	97
STOP AND SMELL THE ROSES	98	93	78	78

TOTALS	BB	CB	RW	'BEST'
TOTAL albums released: 9				
TOTAL albums charted	9	9	9	9
NUMBER ONE albums	0	1	1	1

TOTALS	BB	CB	RW	'BEST'
TOP TEN albums	2	2	2	2
TOP TWENTY albums	2	2	3	3
TOP FIFTY albums	5	5	5	5
TOP 100 albums	7	8	7	8
TOP 200 albums	9	9	9	9

Record World ceased publication just prior to the release of TUG OF WAR.

A Special Note on the Beatles and the American Charts

The lasting popularity of the Beatles and their music over the previous twenty years in America can perhaps be best exemplified by the following facts.

On March 13, 1964, the Beatles placed singles in the top four slots of the *Cash Box* chart, remarkably holding down No. 1 ("She Loves You"), No. 2 ("I Want to Hold Your Hand"), No. 3 ("Please Please Me"), and No. 4 ("Twist and Shout") all in a single week.

They soon topped this feat on April 4, 1964, by securing the top five singles on *Billboard's* chart in the same week, unbelievably commanding the No. 1 ("Can't Buy Me Love"), No. 2 ("Twist and Shout"), No. 3 ("She Loves You"), No. 4 ("I Want to Hold Your Hand") and No. 5 ("Please Please Me") positions (while on the album chart, they held the No. 1 and No. 2 slots with MEET THE BEATLES and INTRODUCING THE BEATLES). In addition, they had a total of twelve entries (A and B sides of eight separate singles) that week on the singles chart. The following week they placed an unbelievable fifteen entries (A and B sides of ten separate singles) on the *Billboard* chart, with fourteen of those in the Top 100.

At the start of 1965, the *Billboard* album chart listed no fewer than eight different Beatles albums in the Top 200 simultaneously, with three of those in the Top Ten, and one of them sitting in the Number One position.

In addition to their record-breaking number of Number One singles and albums, there have been several records that came close, rising to the No. 2 and sometimes No. 3 positions. In almost every instance, they were kept from hitting the Number One position *only* by another Beatles record already there. In the same vein, they replaced themselves with the Number One entry on several occasions, both as a group and as solo artists, providing back-to-back uninterrupted Beatles chart toppers on both the album and singles charts.

In the week immediately following the untimely death of John Lennon, the public rush for Lennon and Beatles product led to the most amazing chart placement ever on America's album charts: By the end of January 1981, there were no fewer than eighteen Beatles-related (group/solo) albums in the Top 200. *Record World* led the way by charting all eighteen albums, among which were eleven by the Beatles, six by John Lennon, and one by Paul McCartney. *Billboard* charted fourteen albums, with seven by the Beatles, six by Lennon, and one by McCartney. *Cash Box* placed a total of eleven albums in their chart, with seven by the Beatles, and four by Lennon. Topping the charts during this period was John and Yoko's DOUBLE FANTASY.

Since their career in the United States began, the Beatles have had more Number One singles than any other artist. First, they managed twenty-three as a group, followed by another twenty as solo artists (ten for McCartney/Wings, four each by Lennon and Starr, and Harrison with two), giving the group and its members a combined all-time record-setting total of forty-three Number One U.S. singles.

On the album charts, the Beatles hit Number One no fewer than eighteen times as a group, as well as an additional fourteen times as solo artists (led by McCartney/Wings with seven, three each for Lennon and Harrison, and one by Starr), giving them a grand total of thirty-two Number One albums in the United States.

THE NUMBER ONE SINGLES

	BB	CB	RW
1. I WANT TO HOLD YOUR HAND/Beatles	1	1	1
2. SHE LOVES YOU/Beatles	1	1	1
3. TWIST AND SHOUT/Beatles	2	1	1
4. CAN'T BUY ME LOVE/Beatles	1	1	1
5. LOVE ME DO/Beatles	1	1	1
6. A HARD DAY'S NIGHT/Beatles	1	1	1
7. I FEEL FINE/Beatles	1	1	1
8. EIGHT DAYS A WEEK/Beatles	1	1	1
9. TICKET TO RIDE/Beatles	1	1	1
10. HELP!/Beatles	1	1	1
11. YESTERDAY/Beatles	1	1	1
12. WE CAN WORK IT OUT/Beatles	1	1	1
13. NOWHERE MAN/Beatles	3	2	1
14. PAPERBACK WRITER/Beatles	1	1	1
15. YELLOW SUBMARINE/Beatles	2	1	1
16. PENNY LANE/Beatles	1	1	1
17. ALL YOU NEED IS LOVE/Beatles	1	1	1
18. HELLO GOODBYE/Beatles	1	1	1
19. HEY JUDE/Beatles	1	1	1
20. GET BACK/Beatles	1	1	1
21. SOMETHING/COME TOGETHER/Beatles	1	1	1
22. LET IT BE/Beatles	1	1	1

ALBUMS	BB	CB	RW
23. LONG AND WINDING ROAD/Beatles	1	1	1
24. MY SWEET LORD/Harrison	1	1	1
25. IT DON'T COME EASY/Starr	4	1	1
26. UNCLE ALBERT/ADMIRAL HALSEY/McCartney	1	1	1
27. IMAGINE/Lennon	3	2	1
28. MY LOVE/McCartney	1	1	1
29. GIVE ME LOVE/Harrison	1	1	1
30. LIVE AND LET DIE/McCartney	2	1	1
31. PHOTOGRAPH/Starr	1	1	1
32. YOU'RE SIXTEEN/Starr	1	1	1
33. BAND ON THE RUN/McCartney	1	1	1
34. WHATEVER GETS YOU THRU THE NIGHT/Lennon	1	1	1
35. NO NO SONG/Starr	3	1	3
36. LISTEN TO WHAT THE MAN SAID/McCartney	1	1	1
37. SILLY LOVE SONGS/McCartney	1	1	1
38. LET 'EM IN/McCartney	3	1	4
39. WITH A LITTLE LUCK/McCartney	1	1	1
40. COMING UP/McCartney	1	2	3
41. (JUST LIKE) STARTING OVER/Lennon	1	1	1
42. WOMAN/Lennon	2	1	2
43. EBONY AND IVORY/McCartney	1	1	

THE NUMBER ONE ALBUMS

	BB	CB	RW
1. MEET THE BEATLES/Beatles	1	1	1
2. INTRODUCING THE BEATLES/Beatles	2	2	1
3. THE BEATLES SECOND ALBUM/Beatles	1	1	1
4. A HARD DAY'S NIGHT/Beatles	1	1	1
5. BEATLES '65	1	1	1
6. BEATLES VI/Beatles	1	1	1
7. HELP!/Beatles	1	1	1
8. RUBBER SOUL/Beatles	1	1	1
9. YESTERDAY . . . AND TODAY/Beatles	1	1	1
10. REVOLVER/Beatles	1	1	1
11. SGT. PEPPER'S LONELY HEARTS CLUB BAND/Beatles	1	1	1
12. MAGICAL MYSTERY TOUR/Beatles	1	1	1

ALBUMS	BB	CB	RW
13. THE BEATLES ("White Album")/Beatles	1	1	1
14. ABBEY ROAD/Beatles	1	1	1
15. HEY JUDE (The Beatles Again)/Beatles	2	2	1
16. McCARTNEY/McCartney	1	1	1
17. LET IT BE/Beatles	1	1	1
18. ALL THINGS MUST PASS/Harrison	1	1	1
19. IMAGINE/Lennon	1	1	1
20. CONCERT FOR BANGLA DESH/Harrison	2	2	1
21. THE BEATLES 1962–1966/Beatles	3	1	4
22. THE BEATLES 1967–1970/Beatles	1	2	1
23. RED ROSE SPEEDWAY/McCartney	1	1	1
24. LIVING IN THE MATERIAL WORLD/Harrison	1	1	1
25. RINGO/Starr	2	1	1
26. BAND ON THE RUN/McCartney	1	1	1
27. WALLS AND BRIDGES/Lennon	1	1	1
28. VENUS AND MARS/McCartney	1	1	1
29. WINGS AT THE SPEED OF SOUND/McCartney	1	1	1
30. WINGS OVER AMERICA/McCartney	1	2	3
31. DOUBLE FANTASY/Lennon	1	1	1
32. TUG OF WAR/McCartney	1	1	*

*Record World ceased publication just prior to the release of TUG OF WAR.

APPENDIX

III

WORLDWIDE QUICK-REFERENCE CHART SUPPLEMENTS

Many countries throughout the world compile record charts, whether it be weekly, biweekly, or even monthly. They range from a basic Top Ten listing to a full scale Top 100 or more. These charts may come from official government sources (e.g., government-controlled radio stations) or private ones (e.g., independent national or local radio stations, music publications, or record shops).

The tremendous success attained by the Beatles and the individual members in the United States as reflected by the chart figures has now been documented in this book. In this section, the international success of the Fab Four will be documented by providing the chart totals for two very important countries in the Beatles' history: England and West Germany.

ENGLAND

There are many similarities between England and America in the record charts and success of the Beatles and the group's individual members. As does the United States, England utilizes three major charts: the *British Market Research Bureau* Top 100 singles and albums charts are used as the basis for the weekly Top 50 singles and albums charts featured in *Music & Video Week;* and the music journals *Melody Maker* and *New Musical Express* each publish their own weekly Top 30 singles and albums charts (though it should be pointed out that the UK charts are based solely on record sales, and do not reflect radio airplay as do their American counterparts).

While it comes as no surprise to find that the group's releases in the sixties achieved virtually identical success in both countries, it is also interesting to note that most of the solo work of the seventies followed similar ups and downs on both sides of the Atlantic. There have however been a few notable exceptions, particularly with some of McCartney's solo singles.

Singles

THE BEATLES	M&VW/ BMRB	MM	NME	"BEST"
LOVE ME DO	17	21	27	17
PLEASE PLEASE ME	2	1	1	1
FROM ME TO YOU	1	1	1	1

THE BEATLES	M&VW/ BMRB	MM	NME	'BEST'
SHE LOVES YOU	1	1	1	1
I WANT TO HOLD YOUR HAND	1	1	1	1
CAN'T BUY ME LOVE	1	1	1	1
A HARD DAY'S NIGHT	1	1	1	1
I FEEL FINE	1	1	1	1
TICKET TO RIDE	1	1	1	1
HELP!	1	1	1	1
WE CAN WORK IT OUT/DAY TRIPPER	1	1	1	1
PAPERBACK WRITER	1	1	1	1
YELLOW SUBMARINE/ELEANOR RIGBY	1	1	1	1
PENNY LANE/STRAWBERRY FIELDS FOREVER	2	1	2	1
ALL YOU NEED IS LOVE	1	1	1	1
HELLO GOODBYE	1	1	1	1
LADY MADONNA	1	2	1	1
HEY JUDE	1	1	1	1
GET BACK	1	1	1	1
BALLAD OF JOHN AND YOKO	1	1	1	1
SOMETHING/COME TOGETHER	4	4	5	4
LET IT BE	2	3	3	2
YESTERDAY	8	4	5	4
BACK IN THE U.S.S.R.	19	18	18	18
SGT. PEPPER'S LONELY HEARTS CLUB BAND/ WITH A LITTLE HELP FROM MY FRIENDS	63	—	—	63
also				
MY BONNIE (w/ Tony Sheridan)	48	38	—	38
AIN'T SHE SWEET	29	24	24	24
SWEET GEORGIA BROWN (w/ T. Sheridan)	—	—	—	—
WHY (w/ Tony Sheridan)	—	—	—	—
TWIST AND SHOUT/FALLING IN LOVE AGAIN	—	—	—	—

EP's

Note—BMRB positions shown are from their Top 20 (changed to Top 10 in 1966) EP chart, which was separate from their singles chart.

Melody Maker and New Musical Express figures show the peak positions attained on their singles charts.

THE BEATLES	M&VW/ BMRB	MM	NME
TWIST AND SHOUT	1	2	4
THE BEATLES HITS	1	14	17
BEATLES No. 1	2	19	24
ALL MY LOVING	1	12	13
LONG TALL SALLY	1	14	11
A HARD DAY'S NIGHT (film extracts)	1	34	—
A HARD DAY'S NIGHT (album extracts)	7	—	—
BEATLES FOR SALE	1	—	—
BEATLES FOR SALE No. 2	5	—	—
MILLION SELLERS (GOLDEN DISCS)	1	—	—
YESTERDAY	1	—	—
NOWHERE MAN	4	—	—
MAGICAL MYSTERY TOUR (double EP)	2*	1	2

also

MY BONNIE (w/Tony Sheridan)	—	—	—

*Peak position attained on singles chart

Singles

JOHN LENNON (w/PLASTIC ONO BAND; YOKO ONO)	M&VW/ BMRB	MM	NME	'BEST'
GIVE PEACE A CHANCE	2	2	2	2
COLD TURKEY	14	12	13	12
INSTANT KARMA	5	4	5	4
POWER TO THE PEOPLE	7	6	6	6
HAPPY XMAS (WAR IS OVER)	4	10	2	2
MIND GAMES	26	23	19	19
WHATEVER GETS YOU THRU THE NIGHT	36	—	24	24
#9 DREAM	23	23	23	23
STAND BY ME	30	—	27	27
IMAGINE	6	5	5	5
(JUST LIKE) STARTING OVER	1	1	1	1

JOHN LENNON (w/PLASTIC ONO BAND; YOKO ONO)	M&VW/ BMRB	MM	NME	'BEST'
IMAGINE (post-death re-entry)	1	1	1	1
HAPPY XMAS (post-death re-entry)	2	3	—	2
WOMAN	1	2	2	1
WATCHING THE WHEELS	30	—	27	27
also				
GOD SAVE US/DO THE OZ (Elastic Oz Band)	—	—	—	—
28th NOVEMBER 1974 (EP) (w/Elton John)	40	28	24	24

PAUL McCARTNEY (w/WINGS; LINDA McCARTNEY)	M&VW/ BMRB	MM	NME	'BEST'
ANOTHER DAY	2	2	2	2
BACK SEAT OF MY CAR	39	—	—	39
GIVE IRELAND BACK TO THE IRISH	16	18	13	13
MARY HAD A LITTLE LAMB	9	6	6	6
HI HI HI/C MOON	5	5	3	3
MY LOVE	9	10	7	7
LIVE AND LET DIE	9	8	7	7
HELEN WHEELS	12	11	12	11
JET	7	4	6	4
BAND ON THE RUN	3	2	3	2
JUNIOR'S FARM	16	16	16	16
LISTEN TO WHAT THE MAN SAID	6	6	6	6
LETTING GO	41	—	—	41
VENUS AND MARS/ROCK SHOW	—	—	—	—
SILLY LOVE SONGS	2	2	1	1
LET 'EM IN	2	1	2	1
MAYBE I'M AMAZED	28	20	27	20
MULL OF KINTYRE/GIRL'S SCHOOL	1	1	1	1
WITH A LITTLE LUCK	5	6	7	5
I'VE HAD ENOUGH	42	—	—	42
LONDON TOWN	60	—	—	60
GOODNIGHT TONIGHT	5	4	6	4
OLD SIAM, SIR	35	—	27	27
GETTING CLOSER/BABY'S REQUEST	60	—	—	60
WONDERFUL CHRISTMASTIME	6	13	16	6
COMING UP	2	2	2	2
WATERFALLS	9	8	7	7

PAUL McCARTNEY (w/WINGS; LINDA McCARTNEY)	M&VW/ BMRB	MM	NME	'BEST'
TEMPORARY SECRETARY (12-inch)	—	—	—	—
EBONY AND IVORY	1	1	1	1

also

	M&VW/ BMRB	MM	NME	'BEST'
SEASIDE WOMAN (Suzy and Red Stripes)	—	—	—	—
WALKIN IN THE PARK WITH ELOISE (The Country Hams)	—	—	—	—

GEORGE HARRISON	M&VW/ BMRB	MM	NME	'BEST'
MY SWEET LORD	1	1	1	1
BANGLA-DESH	10	12	10	10
GIVE ME LOVE	8	7	8	7
DING DONG; DING DONG	38	—	—	38
DARK HORSE	—	—	—	—
YOU	38	29	—	29
THIS GUITAR	—	—	—	—
THIS SONG	—	—	—	—
TRUE LOVE	—	—	—	—
IT'S WHAT YOU VALUE	—	—	—	—
BLOW AWAY	51	—	—	51
LOVES COMES TO EVERYONE	—	—	—	—
FASTER	—	—	—	—
ALL THOSE YEARS AGO	13	8	9	8
TEARDROPS	—	—	—	—

RINGO STARR	M&VW/ BMRB	MM	NME	'BEST'
IT DON'T COME EASY	4	5	5	4
BACK OFF BOOGALOO	2	3	2	2
PHOTOGRAPH	8	5	4	4
YOU'RE SIXTEEN	4	3	4	3
ONLY YOU	28	26	—	26
SNOOKEROO/OO-WEE	—	—	—	—
OH MY MY/NO NO SONG	—	—	—	—
A DOSE OF ROCK 'N' ROLL	—	—	—	—
DROWNING IN THE SEA OF LOVE	—	—	—	—
TONIGHT/HEART ON MY SLEEVE	—	—	—	—
WRACK MY BRAIN	—	—	—	—

Albums

THE BEATLES	M&VW/ BMRB	MM	NME	'BEST'
PLEASE PLEASE ME	1	1	1	1
WITH THE BEATLES	1	1	1	1
A HARD DAY'S NIGHT	1	1	1	1
BEATLES FOR SALE	1	1	1	1
HELP!	1	1	1	1
RUBBER SOUL	1	1	1	1
REVOLVER	1	1	1	1
A COLLECTION OF OLDIES	7	4	6	4
SGT. PEPPER'S LONELY HEARTS CLUB BAND	1	1	1	1
THE BEATLES ("WHITE ALBUM")	1	1	1	1
YELLOW SUBMARINE	3	4	3	3
ABBEY ROAD	1	1	1	1
LET IT BE	1	1	1	1
THE BEATLES 1962–1966	3	1	1	1
THE BEATLES 1967–1970	2	1	1	1
ROCK 'N' ROLL MUSIC	11	11	10	10
THE BEATLES TAPES	45	—	—	45
LIVE AT THE STAR CLUB IN HAMBURG, GERMANY, 1962	—	—	27	27
BEATLES AT THE HOLLYWOOD BOWL	1	3	1	1
LOVE SONGS	7	12	12	7
RARITIES	71	—	—	71
BALLADS	17	26	21	17

JOHN LENNON (w/PLASTIC ONO BAND; YOKO ONO)	M&VW/ BMRB	MM	NME	'BEST'
TWO VIRGINS	—	—	—	—
LIFE WITH THE LIONS	—	—	—	—
WEDDING ALBUM	—	—	—	—
LIVE PEACE IN TORONTO 1969	—	—	—	—
JOHN LENNON/PLASTIC ONO BAND	11	8	13	8
IMAGINE	1	1	1	1
SOMETIME IN NEW YORK CITY	11	13	19	11
MIND GAMES	13	6	9	6
WALLS AND BRIDGES	6	8	5	5
ROCK 'N' ROLL	6	10	10	6

JOHN LENNON (w/PLASTIC ONO BAND; YOKO ONO)	M&VW/ BMRB	MM	NME	'BEST'
SHAVED FISH	8	5	6	5
DOUBLE FANTASY	1	1	1	1

PAUL McCARTNEY (w/WINGS; LINDA McCARTNEY)	M&VW/ BMRB	MM	NME	'BEST'
McCARTNEY	2	2	2	2
RAM	1	1	1	1
WILD LIFE	11	13	11	11
RED ROSE SPEEDWAY	5	5	4	4
BAND ON THE RUN	1	1	1	1
VENUS AND MARS	1	1	1	1
WINGS AT THE SPEED OF SOUND	2	2	1	1
WINGS OVER AMERICA	8	8	8	8
LONDON TOWN	4	4	4	4
WINGS GREATEST	5	5	3	3
BACK TO THE EGG	6	7	4	4
McCARTNEY II	1	3	1	1
THE McCARTNEY INTERVIEW	34	30	25	25
TUG OF WAR	1	2	1	1

also

	M&VW/ BMRB	MM	NME	'BEST'
CONCERTS FOR THE PEOPLE OF KAMPUCHEA	39	29	—	29

GEORGE HARRISON	M&VW/ BMRB	MM	NME	'BEST'
WONDERWALL MUSIC	—	—	—	—
ELECTRONIC SOUND	—	—	—	—
ALL THINGS MUST PASS	4	1	1	1
CONCERT FOR BANGLA DESH	1	4	4	1
LIVING IN THE MATERIAL WORLD	2	5	3	2
DARK HORSE	—	—	—	—
EXTRA TEXTURE (READ ALL ABOUT IT)	16	20	22	16
BEST OF GEORGE HARRISON	—	—	—	—
THIRTY THREE & 1/3	35	20	25	20
GEORGE HARRISON	39	—	—	39
SOMEWHERE IN ENGLAND	8	8	13	8

RINGO STARR	M&VW/ BMRB	MM	NME	'BEST'
SENTIMENTAL JOURNEY	7	20	15	7
BEAUCOUPS OF BLUES	—	—	—	—
RINGO	7	6	6	6
GOODNIGHT VIENNA	30	—	—	30
BLAST FROM YOUR PAST	—	—	—	—
RINGO'S ROTOGRAVURE	90	—	—	90
RINGO THE 4th	—	—	—	—
BAD BOY	—	—	—	—
STOP AND SMELL THE ROSES	—	—	—	—

also

SCOUSE THE MOUSE (soundtrack)	—	—	—	—

WEST GERMANY

This country is rightfully proud to have served as a vital proving ground for the early Beatles. And once the group had exploded on the international scene, West Germany was one of the countries in which they enjoyed great success, as evidenced by their chart performance on both the single and album charts.

Also interesting is the fact that the group's impressive string of Number One singles began after the Fab Four returned to play a series of concerts in the country in mid-1966. Their triumphant return sparked their popularity to even greater heights, and resulted in several consecutive chart-topping hits.

However, in contrast to the United States and England, where the solo Beatles each went on to maintain a sizable individual success, the individual members did not fare so well on their own in West Germany after the breakup.

The official chart utilized here is from the music trade publication *Der Musikmarkt*, which compiles a weekly Top 75 singles chart and a weekly Top 65 albums chart. These charts are used by a number of other West German music publications.

Singles

THE BEATLES	DM
MY BONNIE	32
TWIST AND SHOUT	10
SHE LOVES YOU	7

THE BEATLES   DM

I WANT TO HOLD YOUR HAND/	1
ROLL OVER BEETHOVEN	31
MISERY	37
KOMM GIB MIR DIENE HAND/	1
SIE LIEBT DICH	7
ALL MY LOVING	32
PLEASE PLEASE ME	20
CAN'T BUY ME LOVE	24
DO YOU WANT TO KNOW A SECRET	34
LONG TALL SALLY	7
PLEASE MR. POSTMAN	47
A HARD DAY'S NIGHT	2
IF I FELL	25
I SHOULD HAVE KNOWN BETTER	6
I FEEL FINE	3
ROCK 'N' ROLL MUSIC	2
EIGHT DAYS A WEEK/	7
NO REPLY	11
TICKET TO RIDE	2
KANSAS CITY	18
HELP!	2
YESTERDAY	6
WE CAN WORK IT OUT	2
MICHELLE	6
NOWHERE MAN	3
PAPERBACK WRITER	1
YELLOW SUBMARINE	1
PENNY LANE	1
ALL YOU NEED IS LOVE	1
HELLO GOODBYE	1
LADY MADONNA	2
HEY JUDE	1
OB-LA-DI OB-LA-DA	1
GET BACK	1
BALLAD OF JOHN AND YOKO	1
SOMETHING/	10
COME TOGETHER	3
LET IT BE	2
LONG AND WINDING ROAD	26
GOT TO GET YOU INTO MY LIFE	22
SGT. PEPPER'S LONELY HEARTS CLUB BAND/	
WITH A LITTLE HELP FROM MY FRIENDS	

JOHN LENNON (w/PLASTIC ONO BAND; YOKO ONO)

	DM
GIVE PEACE A CHANCE	4
COLD TURKEY	—
INSTANT KARMA	11
MOTHER	26
POWER TO THE PEOPLE	7
IMAGINE/IT'S SO HARD	18
HAPPY XMAS (WAR IS OVER)	45
WOMAN IS THE NIGGER OF THE WORLD	—
MIND GAMES	37
WHATEVER GETS YOU THRU THE NIGHT	42
#9 DREAM	—
STAND BY ME	22
YA YA	47
IMAGINE/WORKING CLASS HERO	46
(JUST LIKE) STARTING OVER	4
IMAGINE (post-death re-entry)	7
WOMAN	4
WATCHING THE WHEELS	46

PAUL McCARTNEY (w/WINGS; LINDA McCARTNEY)

	DM
ANOTHER DAY	6
EAT AT HOME	28
UNCLE ALBERT/ADMIRAL HALSEY	30
GIVE IRELAND BACK TO THE IRISH	—
MARY HAD A LITTLE LAMB	—
HI HI HI	16
MY LOVE	43
LIVE AND LET DIE	31
HELEN WHEELS	33
MRS. VANDERBILT	33
JET	6
BAND ON THE RUN	22
JUNIOR'S FARM	—
LISTEN TO WHAT THE MAN SAID	42
LETTING GO	—
VENUS AND MARS/ROCK SHOW	—
SILLY LOVE SONGS	14
LET 'EM IN	29
MAYBE I'M AMAZED	—
MULL OF KINTYRE	1

PAUL McCARTNEY (w/WINGS; LINDA McCARTNEY)	DM
WITH A LITTLE LUCK	17
I'VE HAD ENOUGH	33
LONDON TOWN	33
GOODNIGHT TONIGHT	34
GETTING CLOSER	—
WONDERFUL CHRISTMASTIME	—
COMING UP	12
WATERFALLS	—

GEORGE HARRISON	DM
MY SWEET LORD	1
WHAT IS LIFE	3
BANGLA-DESH	23
GIVE ME LOVE	28
DARK HORSE	46
DING DONG; DING DONG	31
YOU	43
THIS GUITAR	—
THIS SONG	28
CRACKERBOX PALACE	—
BLOW AWAY	—
FASTER	—
ALL THOSE YEARS AGO	—

RINGO STARR	DM
BEAUCOUPS OF BLUES	43
IT DON'T COME EASY	5
BACK OFF BOOGALOO	12
PHOTOGRAPH	5
YOU'RE SIXTEEN	19
OH MY MY	34
ONLY YOU	28
SNOOKEROO/OO-WEE	—
GOODNIGHT VIENNA/NO NO SONG	—
A DOSE OF ROCK'N'ROLL	42
YOU DON'T KNOW ME AT ALL	—
HEY BABY	—
DROWNING IN THE SEA OF LOVE	—

RINGO STARR   DM

SNEAKING SALLY THROUGH THE ALLEY
WRACK MY BRAIN
PRIVATE PROPERTY

Albums

Note—Album chart began in January 1965. Top 50 albums chart 1965–1980. In 1981, became Top 65 album chart.

THE BEATLES	DM
BEATLES FOR SALE	1
SOMETHING NEW	38
YEAH YEAH YEAH (A HARD DAY'S NIGHT)	5
WITH THE BEATLES	34
BEATLES '65	9
BEATLES VI	15
HELP!	1
RUBBER SOUL	1
BEATLES GREATEST	38
YESTERDAY AND TODAY	13
REVOLVER	1
SGT. PEPPER'S LONELY HEARTS CLUB BAND	1
MAGICAL MYSTERY TOUR	8
THE BEATLES ("WHITE ALBUM")	1
YELLOW SUBMARINE	5
ABBEY ROAD	1
LET IT BE	4
THE BEATLES 1962–1966	2
THE BEATLES 1967–1970	2
ROCK 'N' ROLL MUSIC	10
LIVE AT THE STAR CLUB IN HAMBURG, GERMANY, 1962	21
BEATLES AT THE HOLLYWOOD BOWL	10
20 GOLDEN HITS	4

JOHN LENNON (w/PLASTIC ONO BAND; YOKO ONO)	DM
TWO VIRGINS	—
LIFE WITH THE LIONS	—
WEDDING ALBUM	—

JOHN LENNON (w/PLASTIC ONO BAND; YOKO ONO)	DM
LIVE PEACE IN TORONTO 1969	—
JOHN LENNON/PLASTIC ONO BAND	39
IMAGINE	10
SOMETIME IN NEW YORK CITY	—
MIND GAMES	—
WALLS AND BRIDGES	41
ROCK 'N' ROLL	37
SHAVED FISH	—
DOUBLE FANTASY	2

PAUL McCARTNEY (w/WINGS; LINDA McCARTNEY)	DM
McCARTNEY	15
RAM	22
WILD LIFE	47
RED ROSE SPEEDWAY	—
BAND ON THE RUN	15
VENUS AND MARS	11
WINGS AT THE SPEED OF SOUND	32
WINGS OVER AMERICA	8
LONDON TOWN	6
WINGS GREATEST	18
BACK TO THE EGG	16
McCARTNEY II	19

GEORGE HARRISON	DM
WONDERWALL MUSIC	22
ELECTRONIC SOUND	—
ALL THINGS MUST PASS	10
CONCERT FOR BANGLA DESH	29
LIVING IN THE MATERIAL WORLD	20
DARK HORSE	45
EXTRA TEXTURE	—
BEST OF GEORGE HARRISON	—
THIRTY THREE & 1/3	—
GEORGE HARRISON	—
SOMEWHERE IN ENGLAND	36

SENTIMENTAL JOURNEY	—
BEAUCOUPS OF BLUES	—
RINGO	28
GOODNIGHT VIENNA	39
BLAST FROM YOUR PAST	—
RINGO'S ROTOGRAVURE	—
RINGO THE 4th	—
BAD BOY	—
STOP AND SMELL THE ROSES	—

In addition to some of the noticeable differences between the United States and England regarding peak chart positions for certain releases, there have been instances where a record achieved greater success and popularity abroad than in either the United States or England. As noted, while most of the group's hits of the sixties were universal chart toppers, the rule of thumb for much of the seventies seemed to be that if any given release was a hit in America or Britain, it would generally be a hit in most other countries. Of course there were exceptions. However, perhaps of even more interest are a number of records which did in fact gain greater success around the world than in either England or the United States. Some examples:

Wings	"Give Ireland Back to the Irish"	—	#1—Spain; Ireland
Wings	"Mrs. Vanderbilt"	—	#8—Spain
Harrison	"Ding Dong; Ding Dong"	—	#7—Belgium
Lennon	"Stand By Me"	—	#1—South Africa
Wings	"Venus and Mars/Rock Show"	—	#3—Israel
Wings	"Letting Go"	—	#13—Israel
McCartney	"Waterfalls"	—	#7—Israel
			#9—Norway

Additionally, some of the group's reissue albums have performed much better around the world:

Beatles	LIVE AT THE STAR CLUB IN HAMBURG, GERMANY, 1962	—	#8—France
Beatles	LOVE SONGS	—	#9—Portugal
Beatles	RARITIES	—	#10—Canada
Beatles	BALLADS	—	#1—Australia

INDEX

INDEX

ACKNOWLEDGMENTS

Special thanks and acknowledgment is given to the following for their kind cooperation and assistance in providing material for this book:

Billboard—Billboard Publications, Inc., Hollywood and New York
Cash Box—Hollywood and New York
Record World—Record World Publishing Co., Inc., Hollywood and New York
Music & Video Week—London, England
Melody Maker—London, England
New Musical Express—London, England
British Market Research Bureau—London, England
Der Musikmarkt—West Germany

(and the following record companies)

EMI	CBS	Phoenix
Capitol	Columbia	Audio-Fidelity
Apple	Portrait	Silhouette Music
United Artists	Boardwalk	Mobile Fidelity
Warner Brothers	Pickwick International	Sound Labs
Dark Horse	Polydor	Great Northwest
Geffen	M-G-M/Metro	Music Company
Atlantic	Vee Jay	P.B.R. International
Lingasong	Decca	PAC Records
ATCO	Ode	WEA (UK)
Clarion	MCA	RCA (UK)
Sire	K-Tel	
Adam VIII	Hall of Music	

Special thanks to the following individuals who deserve special recognition:

Sid Parnes, Samuel Graham, Suzanne Miller, Carl Skiba, Brian Gelles (Record World) / Sam Sutherland (Billboard/Record World) / Bill Wardlow, Shirley Ladd, Steve Singer (Billboard) / Mel Albert, Harald Taubenreuther (Cash Box) / Mark Lewishon (Music & Video Week) / Pam Sellers (BMRB) / Dave Howling (Melody Maker) / Roy Carr (New Musical Express) / Paul Raxworthy (EMI) / Robert Merlis, Donna Ferguson (Warner Bros.) / Barbara Cook, Patti Hirten, Laurie Wettstein (Columbia) / Pat Britt (Vee Jay) / Don Ellis (RCA-UK) / William Fowler, Sue Foster (WEA-UK) / Michael Macaluso (WEA) / Mike Dion (MFSL) / Len Leonards (Silhouette) / Janet Olmstead, Tanya Campana (Great Northwest Music Co.) / Ed Balder (PAC) / Derrick Havenga, Jack Gergen (Pickwick) / Mike Lefebvre (L/C Distributors) / Skip Olsen (KEZY-AM/FM) / Garry, Mitch, Mike (Blue Meanie Record Shop) / Roger Garceau Photography / Jean, Gary, Kevin, Ed

(The Wherehouse) / Antonio Ferreira, Nelio Rodrigues (Brazil) / Renato Facconi (Italy) / Trevor Hilton (Australia) / Michel Bisson (Canada) / Risty (U.S.A.) / Steve Dunn, Melissa Thomas (The Typecasters) / and Jim Rohrig (BOTH Productions)

Special consultants/coordinators foreign chart data:

Stephen F. D. Baker—England
Willi Braam—West Germany